Travel Portals

Your Passport to Amazing Travel Secrets,

Savings and Stress-Free Trips

By Melvin Harris

Copyright © 2021 Melvin Harris.

All rights reserved. No part of this publication may be reproduced, distributed, or transmitted in any form or by any means, including photocopying, recording, or other electronic or mechanical methods, without the prior written permission of the publisher, except in the case of brief quotations embodied in critical reviews and certain other noncommercial uses permitted by copyright law.

The authors and publisher of this book and the accompanying materials have used their best efforts in preparing this material. The authors and publisher make no representation or warranties with respect to the accuracy, applicability, fitness, or completeness of the contents of this material. They disclaim any warranties expressed or implied, merchantability, or fitness for any particular purpose. The authors and publishers shall in no event be held liable for any loss or other damages, including but not limited to special, incidental, consequential, or other damages. If you have any questions or concerns, the advice of a competent professional should be sought

Some of the links presented in the book might become outdated as their functionality is subjected to their owner's inclinations. In such a case, readers are advised to search for alternatives.

Manufactured in the United States of America

ISBN: 978-1-950576-89-0 (Paperback)

ISBN: 978-1-950576-89-0 (E-Book)

Printed by TBA, in the United States of America.

First printing edition ____.

Preface

Growing up, I always thought about traveling to distant places and exploring various lands and cultures. Even at night, I would gaze up at the stars and dream of how wonderful it would be to journey throughout the universe visiting the planets. I imagined the excitement of being able not only to witness but experience the many places and wonders all around us. As I grew older, that passion to travel continued to burn inside me from each trip I took, no matter what the destination. However, my appetite for travel, while not subsiding, was being pushed into a corner as life has a way of throwing you curve balls and having you juggle many things in your daily routine that ends up putting a lot of stress on your bank account.

Let's face it, no matter if you're looking to take a trip with family, friends or by yourself, travel can be expensive as costs can quickly add up. When speaking with people about travel the reaction I often get is…"how can I afford it" or "I just don't have time or money to travel." I have learned that both of these views are misguided and perpetuate the myth that travel is not affordable or is too expensive. Fortunately, travel doesn't have to cost much; you just need to know how to maximize the value of your trip. Anyone on a budget, including people with a busy lifestyle can, with the correct planning and smart spending, travel more often to see all those destinations on their dream list.

A famous Chinese philosopher, Lao Tzu, once stated that, "The journey of a thousand miles begins with one step." Likewise, desires to fulfill our travel goals or wants require us to take the first step to become unbound by fears of the unknown, excuses, or restrictions presented by our budget. If you are just waiting for things to happen or change, good luck. The simple fact is that daydreaming about your next getaway or lifelong fantasy trip is not enough, you must take action. Wishing to experience a new culture or place is just a hope; you must act by applying knowledge. This is where *Travel Portals* comes in to provide the recipe for you to travel well without compromising, even in lean times. Filled with shrewd strategies and shortcuts for both experienced and newbie travelers, it unlocks the possibilities of you becoming empowered to travel smartly whenever, wherever in the world your dreams take you. Whether you're planning a family reunion, weekend getaway, a relaxing retreat, or seeking to explore a new destination, this is your go-to guide for getting there with ease and without hassles. The information that you will discover in each chapter will have you set to have your best trip yet while saving you time and loads of money.

In the pages that follow, we blended some of the travel industry's best kept secrets for exceptional insider savings and insights for you to travel with confidence and in style.

Go ahead, explore – dream – discover. Let your journey begin.

Melvin Harris

Table of Contents

Preface	3
Introduction	7
Chap. 1: Planning Your Trip – Navigating Travel Options with Ease	12
Chap. 2: How to Find the Best Airfare	33
Chap. 3: Book a Deal Anytime on a Place to Stay	58
Chap. 4: Where to Find Last Minute Travel Bargains	80
Chap. 5: How to Travel for Free	98
Chap. 6: Students and Senior Travel Deals	112
Chap. 7: Stress-Free Family Vacations and Travel	127
Chap. 8: Going Alone – How to Travel Solo and Get the Most Out of Your Trip	155
Chap. 9: Bon Voyage — Score Great Bargains on Overseas Getaways	174
Chap. 10: Fantastic Voyages – Cruise in Style for Less	199
Chap. 11: Smart Safety and Healthy Tips for Worry-Free Travel	213
Chap. 12: Essential Apps to Make Every Journey Easier, Faster, and Hassle-Free	232
Conclusion	239
Index	240
About the Author	248
About Harris Business Enterprises, LLC	249

Introduction

Ah... at last, you are finally — against all odds — taking that much awaited dream vacation. Hearty congratulations to you! Now, in anticipation of your journey, pause just for a brief moment to celebrate by taking a deep breath and picture the sensation of sitting beneath a row of palm trees overlooking a turquoise sea. Feel the extraordinary sensation of a warm tropical breeze coming off the ocean with the magical silhouette of mountains on the horizon beneath a clear sky. Yes — what a wonderful visualization of euphoria to start your journey.

However, along with all the excitement that you feel when the imagery of your destination begins to fade and reality once again resumes prominence, you are also feeling slightly overwhelmed. With your tickets printed and your bags packed as you rush out of your door on the way to the airport, there are a million things going through your mind that you began to think about regarding your trip.

Luckily you no longer have to tackle your travel anxieties and concerns alone. With Travel Portals at your fingertips you can relax, it's here to help you every step of the way. It's filled with resources, savvy tips and keen insights that you can immediately act upon to plan your journey cheaper, safer and stress-free. Following the advice outlined throughout the book is a step in the right direction to ensure that you can enjoy your trip without worry

Look around. You probably know or come across many people who are pondering the possibility of traveling, whether to a sought after destination or visit far away family or friends but don't think such a journey is easily affordable. Let's get one thing straight—this book is not about putting off travel until you have everything lined up such as the kids' finishing school, you winning the lottery, or you don't have a traveling companion when the urge to go hits you. Unlike other travel books that will tell you where to go and what to do, Travel Portals is your passport to how to travel well for a fraction of the going rate. So, even with a tight budget forget about waiting until next year as you now have the information you'll need to leave nothing but footprints at all the wonderful places you'll visit.

While this book is not a guidebook by any means, it is a reference tool. Being a traveler myself, I know first-hand how frustrating and time consuming it can be to uncover incredible specials on airfares, hotels, cruises, restaurants, and more when you are planning a trip. That's why Travel Portals make it easy for you to save time, money and hassles so you don't have to click through endless searches to get the information you'll need to get the best deals. Open this book to read any chapter and you'll discover insightful tips that help you in your journey

I fully understand that the needs of every traveler vary. I have written this book for both the infrequent and experienced travelers who could benefit on ways to travel smart and save, without lowering their standards. So, wherever you are in your travel journey if:

- You are a first-timer traveler who is looking to find travel deals for less and needs comprehensive guidance on trip planning while embarking on your first vacation. You need guidance to avoid 'most common' mistakes and travel hacks right off the bat.
- You are an experienced traveler but are busy and looking to save time on planning your trip. You just need quick advice to make the most of your time once you arrive at the destination.

- You do not wish to plow through an endless list of restaurants and dine-in places when you are on the go. Your focus is rather on memorable experiences that you will remember long after coming back from vacation.
- You are considering a cruise and want information on how best to save.
- You are traveling solo and looking for advice for how to make the most of being on the road alone.
- You are traveling with family and need guidance on keeping it safe yet entertaining for the kids.

If any of these criteria fit your description or you are looking to save on your next trip, then this book is just for you!

Moving Forward!

The world is your oyster. Think of Travel Portals as your constant companion. The chapters that follow will offer helpful hints, insider tips, and strategies that I have compiled during my research and travels. I explored, took notes, and made a ton of mistakes but also learned from them. I do not wish others to repeat my mistakes regardless of whether you are a first-timer or a seasoned traveler.

From here on, you may head towards your holiday destination. The world is at your feet and everything in this book will help you make your travels a memory worth cherishing for years on-end. You will make new friends, visit mesmerizing locations, and have experiences worth sharing with others.

Bon voyage!

Chapter 1: Planning Your Trip – Navigating Travel Options with Ease

Planning a trip can be nothing short of overwhelming even for seasoned travelers. There are a tons of questions and variables to tackle. Where to begin? What is step one? What to do once you arrive? How to leave in case of an emergency? Suffice to say, traveling more is something many of us want to do but it can be filled with anxiety, especially if it is something that you do infrequently or you are an occasional traveler who would love adventure or like to experience new places.

There could be a range of reasons because why you may not have had gotten around to a trip of your lifetime. Needless to say, I am here to make that process a breeze for you!

Regardless of whether you are a solo traveler, someone taking a much-awaited family vacation or you just need an escape from the urban lifestyle, sorting through multiple options for hotel stays, in addition to landing convenient airfare, train or bus schedules can be exhausting as well as frustrating when you're looking to find great deals to save. Far from the madding crowd, it's time to create priceless memories for you and your family. A few decades from now, you will cherish these unforgettable moments.

All of this can be achieved without enduring the hassle of planning a trip. Call it a travel options checklist, if you may.

For the uninitiated, this chapter will guide you on smooth but easy travel planning and all the considerations that you need to take. Following this checklist will ensure that you have everything planned to the last detail.

Okay, let's dive right in on some ways to travel smart:

1. *Selection of Destination*

It is time to bite the bullet. Which travel destination is on your mind that suits your travel budget and interests?

Whether you are opting for a domestic trip or an overseas escape, the whole purpose of a vacation is to relax and have an enjoyable time. It is about taking your mind off of the conventional worries.

2. *Time of the Trip?*

If your vacation period is only about 1 to 2 weeks each year, you don't want to spend most of the time reaching and coming back from the destination. It is key to plan out the trip accordingly. Even for a quick weekend getaway, some advanced preparation is essential to experience an enjoyable journey.

On the other hand, if you have more time, say 2 to 4 weeks or even a month for that matter, you can definitely plan a great trip out of the country.

3. *Who are your traveling companions?*

Before you go about selecting a travel destination, you need to keep in mind the travel companions you are doing along with. A great deal of your choices can be affected due to the traveling companions and their personal likes/dislikes.

Traveling solo or, with a family or as a couple? The choices greatly differ for all three options.

Have a meeting with the traveling companions and shortlist their interests and ideas about the trip. Memorable trips are ones where everyone enjoys something they like. Remember to democratize the trip. Everyone needs to have a say in this and this is how they have all have something to look forward to.

4. What Should an Ideal Trip Have?

Select a destination that offers the maximum benefits for you to enjoy. These can include a mix of the below:

- Road trips
- Resorts
- Culture and festivals
- Winter and summer seasons
- Mountains and beaches
- Adventure and relaxation
- Shopping extravaganza and culinary delights
- Budget, mid-range and luxury options

Options really matter and on a personal level, reading a book by the poolside may be your thing to relax but is a big no-no for others. Find options that matter most to you so you can have a memorable trip rather than a one that is forgettable.

Keep an open mind. The options are as many -as you want and as needless as you perceive them to be.

5. *When to Travel*

Crowd and weather both play a contributory role in planning a trip. Check out the busy season and low season in your targeted destination. You are in luck if you can squeeze in a spot in high-traffic season, though peak travel periods are not really advised.

6. *Calculate Your Overall Costs*

Now that you have decided about the travel destination and the duration of your stay, it is time to crunch those numbers. You need to calculate the cost of doing this trip and coming back with some loose change. The cost will determine the mode of travel and feature-filled vacations that you can work with. You need to gauge the pricing of option for backpacks or luxury hotels. The attractions, hotels, restaurants and hostels are all something that you will need take into account. When you have factored these bare essentials, a map will start to emerge about your standing on this trip.

Let's make this a tad bit easier:

- Start with a guidebook (or conduct an internet search for a free travel guide or information about your destination)
- Ask around and indulge in opinion-sharing from Facebook groups, Lonely Planet and others
- Check out the prices of the facilities and other things you have in mind

That is the long and short of it. Avoid over-planning as this can muddle up the trip and the barrage of available information is too much to take as it is. Stick to these three and you are almost there.

For instance, in a 10-day trip to Paris, you will need only $75 per day (excluding the flight expenses) so you will have $800 ideally. Budget trips are so much light on the pocket. Now that you have a plan, you can work around it or still save some while on the way back.

The overall expenditure of a trip depends on the number of days you plan to spend and amount of activities you want to get done.

7. *Book your Accommodation, Pronto!*

A major travel expenditure is where you sleep. Thus, choosing an accommodation that suits your needs at a price you desire can free up some extra cash for other activities.

For those traveling with children, it is really not about the most inexpensive accommodation, but more about the best value for your money on accommodations that meet your needs. As a parent, rough sailing is off the table while during pre-marriage days, it was the go-to option.

Based on the length of the destination and trip, travelers alternate between the accommodation styles. For a solo traveler, apartments are a big yes for the following advantages:

- They have a separate kitchen
- Laundry facility is available
- Separate bedrooms and a living room
- You can live on rent and even split the costs with a family/bunch of friends living there already

These additional amenities in a trip offer a wealth of convenience and drive down costs remarkably. If your stay is a bit briefer, then a hotel will suffice.

If you are a fan of hotels, you can get some sweet deals on them, too. They can cost a pretty penny if you don't properly plan but it pays to have them as an option. For instance, Marriot offers reward points that equal to a one-week stay in the hotel. Similarly, other hotels have terrific offers and there is no shortage of benefits that could help you save.

These 3 booking sites are the best in business for accommodation:

- Booking.com – It is available in 200 countries and has guesthouses, budget hotels and everything in between. They have the best deals on offer and biggest inventory.
- Agoda – It is ideal for Asian market, featuring the best range of properties from this region.
- Hostelworld – It has a huge selection of hostels and attracts a broad range of customers for reliable and affordable hostels.

8. *Look for Viable Accommodation Deals*

As a traveler myself, I advise to book in advance and get the best deal at the time. Look for noteworthy accommodation websites. Some of them have registered properties all over the globe. These accommodation giants are not only listed with the renowned hotel brands, you can also find cozy and low-cost accommodation options to stay the night, week or month depending on your tastes, budget, destination and what kind of comfort you desire.

These websites are a complete package as they have an all-in-one solution for the customers. From hostels, apartments, hotels and holiday homes, they have everything. Furthermore, you can avail seasonal offers and discounts during the holiday season. Read up on the reviews posted by the verified customers and select whichever accommodation strikes your fancy.

Accommodation types to choose from are:

- Guesthouses
- Resorts
- Hotels
- Apartments
- Hostels

AirBnB

During the trip planning, consider Airbnb, they are a lifesaver. A lot of people use Airbnb because they are remarkably affordable. There is a reason the hoteling industry is under threat from this juggernaut. Interestingly enough, the brand is available in 180 countries. You can book entire houses, apartments or even spare bedrooms for that matter. It is all a matter of personal choice.

Mix with the owner and you might also get a free of cost tour of the city and information that is known only by the locals.

9. *Transportation for Moving Around*

One significant aspect to consider while trip planning is to have a bunch of transportation options for your desired destination.

You need to have an open mind to pre-purchase transportation passes or get a rental car when you arrive in the city. Note down the bus service(s) and train that covers the city. If all else fails, there will still be Uber, Lyft or Careem (depending on your location – it is currently operating in 100 cities in the Middle East, Africa and South Asia) to take you to your desired locations. The trend of walking is also common in many nations and you should this in mind.

Fun fact: When you are in Sydney, you will need that Opal Card to use public transportation. It is the same as Oyster Card which is used to access public transportation in London.

Suffice to say, research the available transport options in your targeted city. This saves much-needed time and stress once you arrive.

Rental Cars

To easily get around at your destination sometimes you just need a set of wheels. If you plan to rent a car, its best to book it online well in advance. It is hassle-free and you will surely get a car than just dropping by at their counter. It is quick and easy.

No one wants to haggle with rental car companies after a long flight. It doesn't matter whether you're on a quick weekend getaway or traveling cross-country, one thing for sure everyone can appreciate is saving money when renting a vehicle. So before arriving at the rental car location be sure to do your online research to find the best deal on your next road trip. Use those aggregator websites to quickly browse through the renowned car rental companies operating in the city.

While there is no magic sauce to help you score big when booking a car rental, there are a few helpful tips for the budget conscious traveler that can save you time and money:

- Shop the web:
    - Kayak
    - Hotwire
    - Priceline
    - Cheapcarrental.com
    - Fly.com
- Google for promotions

Google the rental company with the phrase 'promo code". Chances are that you are likely to find a promo or discount code that will get you a better deal. Try – AutoSlash (rental quotes, tracking and coupons), (XX discount codes (generic search), boardingarea.com (search collection of frequent flyer blogs), and FllyerTalk (community forum of frequent flyers) as a source to locate discounts codes.

- Leverage memberships, credit cards and affiliations.

If you belong to AAA, AARP, Costco, a credit union or some other group affiliation be sure to mention it to see if you qualify for a discount.

Some credit cards and rewards programs like American Express and Chase also have benefits that give you access to deals and discounts with certain auto rental services.

- Skip rental car insurance

Chances are that one of the insurance policies that you already hold such as your auto, health, etc. include some type of coverage. Many of credit cards for personal and business already provide this benefit as well if you use your card to pay for the rental. Always check with your card holder or read the policy to ensure you understand the level of coverage they provide.

If you are renting overseas, you might be required to purchase insurance even if you have coverage with your primary car insurance and /or your credit card.

- Consider discount brands

Many rental companies are vying for your business. Don't overlook discount brands like Thrifty, Dollar and Payless Rental who often offer a lower rate than the big-named rental companies. Whatever you decide, keep in mind that certain names in the rental business are renowned and it is prudent to use them in such one-off trips. They know how to handle a tourist and offer them handy tips while they are at it.

10. Checklist of Things to Do and See

Whenever you plan a trip, keep the must-visit tourist attractions (also known as tourist traps) on top of your list. Free activities are aplenty in foreign countries. It pays to have a well thought out strategy when you are heading into a certain travel destination in peak travel season. While you are strapped for time, you also need to complete your to-do list.

For instance, Australia's Sydney Harbor Bridge Climb and Alcatraz prison in San Francisco, California are popular attractions. They are booked well in advance and you would be really pushing your luck if you just show up to get in right away.

Keep the best time to get into the zoos, theme parks and concerts among other things. Other cities offer city passes which saves a few dollars on tourist traps.

In short, it pays to plan!

- Make a checklist and keep the following in mind:

- Famous restaurants in the city
- Tourist traps
- Less renowned landmarks
- Theme parks and concerts happening in the city/area
- Museums and public parks

Make another list separate from the above:

- Day trips
- City tours
- Free of cost activities
- Ideal walks

Internet-based resources are the following where you can fish for new ideas and something that is amiss on your radar:

- Instagram
- Twitter
- Friends and family abroad
- Tourism board websites
- Pinterest
- Travel blogs
- Guide books and city guides

11. Keep the Visa Requirements in Mind

What are the travel visa requirements of your destination? Is a visa required and how flexible are the terms and conditions depending on the country of choice.

As again, all the countries have their respective rules and regulations. Never leave this detail to the last minute. In case you miss out something, you may have to reorganize the entire trip and it could be a preventable hassle.

12. Smart Packing

Packing can be another stressful aspect of trip planning. Sometimes, people leave the hardest things for the last. The best idea is to pack just the bare essentials because you can buy everything from there.

If you have children, pack their clothes but take their opinion as well. No one likes complaining kids, who puts extra stress on the entire trip.

The clothes really depend on the weather of the location at hand. Try to be as casual as possible. The more casual wear you have, the more expendable it is. At times, some clothes can get dirty and you can always replace them with a cheaper alternative.

Packing cells are just amazing for budget trips. Each compartment has space for a particular set of item and this way, everything remains in place. Keep the essentials with you like the pajamas, jeans and casual t-shirts.

Pro-tips for packing

You can never go wrong with the list below:

- Find out the weather condition of the targeted location you have in mind. This prevents over-packing.
- Always keep a carry-on case that contains an extra pair of clothes. This is advantageous when checked-in luggage takes time to arrive.
- Keep in mind the activities so as to pack appropriately.
- The facilities offered by the accommodation in question. Don't carry extra baggage if they have it all there already.
- Keep the electronic devices charges and keep entertainment stuff packed in particular spots for quick access.

13. Keep Copies of Vital Documents

During trip planning and everything in between, valuable documents can get misplaced and this can cause chaos. Moreover, companies can also sometimes lose track of vital customer data and you may get limited service because there is a clear communication gap.

This is why, it is very important to have multiple copies of certain documents. These are the following:

- Hotel reservations
- Itineraries
- Visas
- Passports
- Reservations of rental cars
- Driver's license
- Credit cards
- Tour bookings
- Other information you may need there

Have hard copies and save all this essential data in emails in order to retrieve with ease when urgently required. Leave the original copies at home in hands of a trustworthy person. If multiple companies are on the trip, then each of them should have a copy. Hardcopies are really necessary because internet and email may not be available in remote areas.

At times, even the immigration authorities lose passports of customers and this is why hardcopies can come in handy. It fast-tracks the processing and ensures that your schedule remains untainted.

14. Remember to Immunize

For those travelers (especially with young children) heading to overseas destinations, this step is crucial to prevent unwarranted medical expenses. Depending on the location at hand, it is vital to be properly vaccinated before you land on foreign soil. Health and safety are essential and a sick child/adult leaves a bad taste in everyone's mouth. In some cases, proof of vaccination is required.

Consult an experienced physician, well-aware with necessary precautions during overseas trips. It is advisable to visit these professionals 2-months before because these vaccines take 6 to 8 weeks to fully spread out.

15. Automate Bills Temporarily

Go paperless for the time being. Get rid of the mail and use the online bill payment for monthly. This will ensure that you are not behind any utility bills during your overseas stay. However, this feature is only needed if you are overseas for a few months in a row. A week-long or 14-day trip does not really require this to be done and feel free to skip it.

16. Inform the Credit Card Companies about Traveling

Regardless of the extent of your stays on a foreign land, it is viable to keep the credit card companies in the loop about your presence in another country. This way, all the transactions are safe and avoided from being flagged as fraudulent. The credit card is also less liable to be blocked. Nothing is more aggravating calling up those credit card companies to sort this out when you should be enjoying the vacation of your lifetime.

17. Keep an Eye on Last-Minute Deals

Yes. That old chestnut people often miss. It pays to keep an open mind and an open eye for that matter. Before you book some hotel or reserve a seat on the flight, check deals that may have escaped your notice. Your dream destination might be Paris but Berlin might offer you a chance to save 70% for holidaying over there for a week. Maybe Hawaii has a package deal that allows you to save half of your traveling amount. There are alternate circulating around and you can plan another trip this way.

Check out these websites/apps that offer such deals and you can plan your trip around them, too.

- Scott's Cheap Flights
- The Flight Deal

- Holiday Pirates
- Travelzoo.com
- Lastminutetravel.com
- Secretescapes.com
- Hipmunk.com

Chapter 2: How to Find the Best Airfare

Speaking from personal experience, choosing an airline ticket can be an exhausting and traumatizing experience. Packing bags and other stuff is much more manageable because that is just an uncreative task.

Trying to find the best airfare can be a bit demoralizing if you do not know the way to go about it. You may stumble on a flight that falls in your price range miraculously. But while you are sitting on it, the airfare increases and your dream remains unfulfilled. In another case, you might arrive at your destination much later than you anticipated. This could be due to a few layovers and a night at the airport. You may think that it is far too convenient to book an expensive flight and be done with it. But any seasoned traveler would suggest against it because it gives you less wiggle room in spending money at the destination.

That was before, though. Now, there are a few search engines that makes the job much easier, allowing you make time for other things, too. But the market is pretty dense and you have to navigate through to find something that is worth your while.

Airfare does takes a huge chunk of your traveling costs, after all. So, it is a good idea to find a flight that takes you to your desired city in a price that you want. When you save a few bucks on the airfare, you can invest it on other things. If you opt for the routine airliners, you may not have much room to spend on recreational activities later on.

Therefore, you need to have platforms at your disposal which saves you traveling costs by giving you options. All you need to do is find them. Then again, this chapter does that for you. Some people have made it a point (and career) to find the best deals on airfare available in the market. Whenever they land on such airfare deals, they send it immediately at their mailing lists.

Traveling is all about playing it smart and making the most of what you have. So, if you really like keeping more money in your pocket, this chapter will unveil all the travel hacks people have been using for years to get discounted and affordable flights. Apart from flights, certain ideas slash airfare further when used at the right time.

Let's explore ways to find best airfare that suits you:

1. *Steer Clear of the Myths*

First and foremost, there are a lot of circulating myths about inexpensive flights and ways to get them. They are all false and if you have come across any, simply reject them. They will lead you nowhere at all. It is simply because websites have content writers and reporters that reuse outdated and common myths. Some of these are very common and it is advised to take them with a grain of salt. Listed below are some (not all):

- It is comparatively affordable to purchase airfare on a Tuesday.
- Searching for flights in incognito mode leads to affordable deals.
- There is simply no specific time and date on which airfare should be booked.
- You cannot accurately rely on websites that predict airline prices

The airlines use pricing algorithms and other sophisticated methods to set price points and run sales. This depends on the passenger demand, time of the season, events/festivals, weather, day/time, price of competitors and so much more. The days for those tricks are long gone and they are just a figment of someone's imagination. The system has gotten too smart.

Tune out conversations that are based on this subject. It is really a no-brainer to lend an ear in this day and age.

2. Flexibility in Time and Dates for Travel

The price of an airline ticket is subject to time of the year, week, day, holiday season and other tour-related aspects. For instance, August is huge month for tourism in Europe when school is out and families look for a trip somewhere. Europeans usually look for a warmer climate during this season.

When you are flying in a jam-packed season, then the ticket is obviously going to cost a lot more than in off-season. So, it pays to be flexible with the dates. If you intend to go to Paris, do it in fall or spring when airfares and footfall is remarkably low.

Similarly, you are likely to be out of luck if you wish to fly to Paris in August and Hawaii during Christmas.

Choose off-season for trips.

A common rule of thumb is to book weekday flights compared to weekends. Airlines hike the weekend flights intentionally because passengers choose this out of convenience. Airline fare is cheaper when the flights are late-night ones, when a flight is chosen after a major holiday and early-morning flights since less people prefer to fly at those times.

A one-day difference can mean you can save around hundreds of bucks. Airlines simply make the most of major holiday seasons, sporting event or school break and it makes sound sense as a business decision to raise prices.

Play it smart and save by the bucket load.

3. *Flexibility in Destination Selection*

If you find it hard to be flexible on the dates on which you need to fly, then be flexible about the destination at least. It is ideal to be both, but if you really intend to save your hard-earned money and avail a low-cost flight, then pick either of the two.

The airline search engines have it remarkably easy to look at the whole world and find a ticket that is worth your while. You do not need to search manually either. Kayak has this brilliant option of Explore which allows you to check out all the flights around the world on a virtual map. Google Flights has a comparable but a better feature for the users. You can use these tools to check out a location that is feasible.

4. *Fly on Budget Airlines*

A few decades ago, if you wanted to land on countries located in multiple continents, you were stuck mostly with the conventional and pricey airlines. That is no longer the case. The arrival of budget airlines on the market allows passengers to fly all over the world on a paltry budget. The Norwegian Air Shuttle makes it possible to fly from Europe to Bangkok for just $250, one side.

On the other hand, AirAsia has crazy, low-cost deals for Australia and Asia, that makes it easy on your travel budget. Middle-eastern and Indian airlines are another viable option to take if you plan to spend your vacation in these regions. A budget airline can fly you anywhere around the world in a price range that suits you.

Following is the list of some famous budget airlines passengers' use:

Australia

- Tiger Air
- Jetstar

Europe

- Wizz Air
- Norwegian Air
- Flybe
- Eurowings
- Aigle Azur
- Vueling
- Easyjet
- Ryanair

Asia

- Scoot
- Hong Kong Express
- Air Asia
- Jeju Air
- Jetstar

- <u>Peach Air</u>
- <u>Spice Jet</u>
- <u>T'Way Airlines</u>
- <u>Nok Air</u>
- <u>Spring Airlines</u>

USA

- <u>Frontier</u>
- <u>Allegiant Air</u>
- <u>Southwest</u>
- <u>Spirit Airlines</u>
- <u>Sun Country Airlines</u>

Canada

- <u>Porter</u>
- <u>Air Transat</u>
- <u>Air Canada Rouge</u>
- <u>Swoop</u>
- <u>Flair Airlines</u>

New Zealand

- <u>Jetstar</u>

Do check out the destinations of these budget airlines on their website to shortlist the one that suits you.

These budget airlines may not give you the benefits and convenience offered by the big airliners, but they certainly gets the job done. Consider it as a tradeoff since you cannot have it both ways.

The budget airlines earn on everything that is additional. For instance, the extra luggage, carry-ons, checked bags, printing the boarding pass, credit card and everything in between.

Pro-tip: Compare the total cost with that of a noteworthy carrier.

5. *Never Fly Directly*

If you can be flexible with the dates and times on which you intend to fly, you'll have a much easier time finding some amazing flight deals. Better yet, if you are also open to the idea of being a bit flexible with the route as well you can discover even more opportunities to save. For instance, it is comparatively inexpensive to reach London and take a low-cost airline to Amsterdam city than to directly reach Amsterdam from your location.

There are literally tons and tons of low-carriers and surely, you can find one that reaches your target destination. It saves you quite a bit of cash if you do this for a round trip. Here is something from 'personal experience'. I wanted to board a flight to Paris that was $894. However, after a little digging for other options I instead booked a $564 flight to London and took a low-cost airline to Paris from there for only $60. The flying time increased but I did save $270 overall.

Here is how I did it: I opened Google Flights and searched the flight prices of my target destination. After determining that, I decided to check out flights from different countries nearby to the same the target destination. For myself, the difference should be significant to take that step. After all, it takes extra time and I might as well save some cash while I am at it.

Airwander makes that easier as well. It shows the budget airlines, stopovers and also compares the prices to find something that is good for you. Google Flights has some limitations, no denying that.

But make sure to have a difference of 3-4 hours at least. This is because if something does go wrong, you can manage the issue during that time and take the flight as planned. It is really on you if you miss the flight due to some reason.

On the other hand, you can save some cash and spend it at the destination of your choice. One issue, it just adds time to your total journey.

6. Search Engines are Different

You should view a number of websites to get the best deal or last-minute that appears on your computer. As is the case, budget carriers are often not listed since they do not wish to pay commission while some websites are not in English. This may result in missing out on key deals that you could have availed (if only you had known about them). Some only entertain major airliners.

Orbitz, Expedia or Kayak does not have rates of Ryanair, AirAsia alongside other budget carriers. Similarly, they do not have obscure foreign airliners on their websites that you can see on Momondo or Skyscanner. Thus, all the websites have certain pros and cons (as is the case with everything else).

There are a few favorites which have less cons and more pros though. Listed below are some of the fine ones from the industry:

- **Momondo** – This is a personal favorite right here. It offers a detailed list of airlines and delivers great results, like 92% of the time.
- **Google Flights** – It shows the flights and price points for multiple destinations.
- **Skyscanner** – Just like Momondo, it looks through all the search results to get you the right one. Skyscanner has a great mobile app and website.

Momondo shows all the major, minor airlines, non-English websites and everything else in its search results. That is what you want, right? All the flights in one place. They are strict on whom to form an alliance with and thus, they have a vast list of bookings for the customers. In all the cases, they have the lowest price of all the websites.

A word of advice: Momondo should be the starting point for you and you can take it from there.

7. Miles and Points Pay (literally!)

Yes, you read that right. Read this **airline rewards programs** and you will know everything. It helps you get free upgrades, free flights and even free companion tickets. Regardless of how much you take the plane, you need to be enrolled in the reward program of the said airline.

For the Americans reading this, take American airlines as they have sweet deals with major companies. Thus, you can earn points on the partner flights. For instance, you can earn points on Singapore Airlines because they have an alliance with United Airlines. Similarly, Air France has an alliance with Delta rewards account.

For those with a credit card, they can earn miles from online shopping, sign up bonus, special offers and even surveys. Some have earned a million miles in just one year --- all of that without using an airline or spending money. This results in access to multiple free flights (business class) with family included. You can think of it as a form of travel hack and make the most of it just as others are right now. Some helpful hyperlinks are listed below for you to get a hang of things:

- How I Earn 1 Million Frequent Flier Miles Every Year
- Is Travel Hacking Really a Scam?
- The Ultimate Guide to Travel Hacking

8. *Special Deals are everywhere*

Well, no one likes a cluttered inbox. But if you wish to save on trips, then do sign up with airline search engines, airlines and other airfare-related websites. You can get great last-minute deals/discounts on certain locations. This is a terrific way to save by boarding a less expensive flight.

These low-cost flights are there for just 24 hours and before you know, they are booked full. People have missed out on a $500 flight to South Africa or $700 flight to Japan (that would normally cost a whopping $1,500).

There are frequent flier bonuses and you can avail business-class tickets free of cost. For these sweet deals, you need to keep an eye on the websites listed below:

- Airfarewatchdog – Terrific for finding deals on American flights

- The Flight Deal – It is great for worldwide flights
- Holiday Pirates – Suitable for European flights
- Scott's Cheap Flights – Perfect for American flight deals
- Secret Flying – Ideal for worldwide flights

9. Go Local if Possible (for obvious reasons)

Admitted, the search engines listed above are terrific, they do often miss out on smaller, domestic carriers. This is the case especially in routes that are less popular or even in remote parts of the world. If you are taking a flight to somewhere no one has heard of, use Google to look for a local airliner.

For instance, LADE Air is a state-owned carrier in Argentina. It offers remarkably low-cost flights to Patagonia. That is something which may not pop out on these abovementioned search engines.

The websites of these smaller carriers may offer exclusive offers, which is something that may not appear in the giant search engines. For instance, if you need to fly somewhere in Western Canada, Hawk Air is a local entity that has deals on a weekly basis.

10. Bypass the Advertised Fares

This might be the worst-kept secret for those associated with the travel industry. The industry finds it preferable to keep this information hidden. The advertised fares are just nonsense and it is wise to just overlook them. The good tickets sell and market on their own. It is as simple as that. For instance, airliners may advertise flights from $600 to $800, but the actual deals that cost $400 are also there.

11. Don't Forget to Book If...

You know the location and when to -go there. In rare cases, the price of an airline ticket drops as the date of departure nears. The budget airlines offers a baseline price for flying somewhere and these tickets sell like hot cakes. The remainder ones then sell at a higher cost. This is the case in Australia and Europe. If you have finalized a location and date to fly, book it right now. There is no time like the present and you will save more now than later.

12. Early Bookings, Better Savings!

The airline fares rises when the date of departure gets closer. However, there is a window for the passengers when airlines decrease the fares depending on demand and time of the year. The ideal time to book a flight to a certain destination is 6 to 8 weeks earlier before the departure. A flight 3 months earlier is also reasonable because you will get a pretty sweet deal than in the peak season (no-brainer, right?).

Cheap flights involves a few factors – being flexible about the destination, timings/dates, when you leave and how you reach the destination. Never spend so much time in browsing flight deals. It does not make sense. Ask a repeat traveler you know and you can save some valuable time in that case.

Follow these tips smartly and you can always find a good deal or two on your flights. No one wants to be overcharged for an airline ticket.

13. Purchase Tickets as Individuals

Avoid this at all costs. Never buy tickets in one go. This single purchase just results in paying extra that you could have saved. Let's say that you have a family of four and select four seats in a row. The airliner will locate four seats in a row and charge the highest ticket price for them. Thus, if seat B is for $300, seat A is for $200 while C and D are for $400, it will charge $400 for all the seats.

As a result, you end up paying extra due to lack of awareness. Always buy seats as a solo traveler. Later on, you can make sure that everyone is together.

14. Purchase Tickets in Foreign Currencies

Let's say for instance that you are a westerner and your currency is pretty strong. In that case, you should look to purchase ticket in the currency of the country you are visiting. For instance, the American dollar is quite strong compared to Australian dollar.

For instance, a one-way trip to New York City from Australia was around $1,000 while the same airliner offered a $600 flight to New Zealand. The booking class was same, the schedule was same and the airliner was also the same. The only difference was the currency. It may not work obviously for people from non-western countries, especially if their currency is not doing well.

Get that no foreign transaction fee card and save yourself from surcharges.

15. *Student Discounts are worth it*

For students that are below 26 years, there are tons of discounts. You can get a knockoff of 20% to 30% on the standard airfare. Flight Center and STA Travel can even help you find a low-cost ticket. Keep this in mind.

This tip is great for students looking for a summer trip together.

16. *Hidden City Ticketing*

Yes, that old chestnut. Travelers have used this little-known trick for so long. The 'hidden city' flight is taken when a city that connects to the desired destination is cheaper than taking a direct flight to the destination. Thus, you just take the inexpensive flight to a connecting city and take the next flight to the desired destination.

This is a bit risky, too. Listed below are some reasons for doing this:

- If the luggage is checked, it could reach the final destination on its own --- For this reason, carry-on luggage is advisable if you plan to take this path.
- The airliner may not allow stepping off the plane --- Some airliners do that, ruining your ulterior motive as a result.
- Airline could detect this and take action --- The consequences are not etched in stone, because people miss flights all-round the year.

Skiplagged was a search engine designed to cater this specifically. Knowing the risks involved, it is advised to proceed with caution.

17. Look for Airline Error and Prices

Sometimes, the airliners post fares that are remarkably affordable given their brand name and usual price points. This could be due to human error, technical glitches or even currency conversion mishaps. If you know the place, you can get some serious discounts on your next ticket.

There are certain ways to find the erroneous airfares. Secret Flying and AirFare Watchdog are some terrific resources to get you started right away. Everything is there in one place and you might be looking at your next destination. Skyscanner is another great resource to get things moving for you. Some people usually take this route to save on hefty airline tickets.

18. Select the Cheapest Flight

Kiwi.com is a great platform for two reasons. If you are in a mood for just wanderlust or know a specific place in mind, it works great in both cases. Select the departure point and it will list down all the countries and prices along with it. The list is categorized in terms of price, allowing you to pick the one which is the cheapest of the lot.

19. Timings

Regardless of how much waiting around and analysis you do, the best time to find a deal really depends on you. You may find tons and tons of internet-based articles that discuss the subject at length. But at the end of it, you have to be the pricing analyst yourself to determine a flight deal that suits your time and budgetary constraints.

Some people opine that booking a flight 7 weeks earlier is the best time to get a great knockoff on flight tickets. This is a broad generalization but a time frame of about 2 months is pretty good to analyze the deals that matches your departure timing and everything in between.

20. Never Book on the Weekend

One pretty handy idea to find a flight deal is to keep an eye on them during weekdays. Actually, the airfares goes way up during the weekends because the fares and traffic is both high. The airfares rise from Friday and starts to drop on Monday and afterwards. Wednesdays and Thursdays are deemed to be the best time to find deals on your preferred destination. This was an observation that was made after looking at the flights over a 6-month period.

21. Booking Early

Now this may sound overly clichéd, but that is because it is. One of the best ways to find a sweet deal is to plan the trip well in advance and hit the iron while it is hot (purchase tickets beforehand). Regardless of whichever deals and discounts pass by, booking early gets you to your destination in time, saves a few bucks and makes the entire experience seamless.

22. Flight Comparison Websites

It makes sound sense to look for flight deals from multiple airline flight comparison websites. This is pretty useful and saves you a precious few bucks on the overall trip. There are many websites that are serving customers in this niche, the likes of which includes Kayak, Momondo and Skyscanner. It will show a list of airlines (regional and international) that will connect you to your desired destination. The competition is cutthroat and make no mistake about it: the airlines go out of their way to stand out from the crowd.

23. Vary the Airlines

Agreed, that taking a return trip from a single airline is much easier and convenient, but you have another thing coming. While your desired airline may have the flight to your destination, you could be in a situation where the seats are booked and you are strapped for time. In such a case (and it is nothing new for that matter), browse through the flights offered by other airlines and those that are connecting flights. You need to be flexible about the timing if you wish to reach the destination in time, but it is worth it.

24. Flexibility Pays

Exploring new cultures and never-before-seen lands is a pretty extraordinary experience. If you have a bit of time on your hands, you can find a good deal, save some bucks and get you a flight of your choosing.

Personally speaking, Skyscanner turned out to be my savior in this case. It has this feature called 'Everywhere' which gives you a chance to explore all that you can. Chances are that you may come across a deal that is not listed elsewhere on the internet and you could be off to a destination which others found inaccessible due to any number of reasons.

Remember to enter the departure airport and check the availability for the whole month and cheapest month options. This is great and if something comes up that suits you, you can plan well in advance without going into the clutter.

Kiwi and Google Flights are other entities in the arena that offers similar functions. Skyscanner is a great option but I will leave the final choice to you.

The flexible you are, the better chances are of you finding a suitable flight deal.

25. The Wondrous Honey Chrome Extension

Actually, Honey collects promotions, coupons and discount codes for the consumers. It is a website on its own, but you can just install the extension on the Google Chrome browser. Now with this extension installed on your browser, you no longer need to comb the web databases for discount codes that would/wouldn't work. If you have a valid code, enter it and see you could get a discount. It is pretty great and people have saved a lot of traveling fare and still found flight deals that suits them.

Yes, there are tons and tons of alternatives, but Honey is quite reliable and it is linked with many other websites, too. One of them is Amazon.

26. Set Alerts

Yes, a lot of people do not have the luxury of idling on the internet, looking for offers. In that case, let them come to you instead. You can set alerts for the promotional offers from the major airliners and get them right in your inbox.

Airfarewatchdog, Google Alerts and Skyscanner, among so many others offer this sweet option. All you have to do is select the destination and date. After that, you will keep receiving alerts on ticket prices. It is very convenient and quite handy for working professionals and other busy bees.

Then there is this mighty useful app called Hopper. It keeps the historical trends in perspective and checks the current prices along the trends. People have saved a few hundred bucks with this app and many more will continue to do so.

You can just enter the requirements of your travel (you can even create multiple alerts as well) and the app will begin sending push notifications to you when the price points differ. The downside of this app is that you will need to plow through tons and tons of weekly emails to get something that you want.

27. Booking and Cancellation Period

The two are pretty much related. As a frequent traveler, you may be no stranger to last-second cancellations. That is your slot to fill in! Wait until the last moment and you may have something up your alley. It works like a charm and it has always happened. In most cases, the cancellation of hotel slots is from 24 to 48 hours. The rooms are also available at discounted prices and that is your cue.

28. Never Shop That Early or That Late

Careful on this one. Book too early and you may pay quite a bit. Book much later on and you will pay much more than you had imagined! The sweet spot for accommodation deals is found, in most cases, in certain time frames. We will lay it out for you.

Tickets for USA: Look for them between 3 months to last 30 days before your expected departure.

International tickets: Look for them between 5 months and last 1 month before your expected departure.

29. Cheapest Flying and Staying Days

You can find accommodations that suit you the same way you look for the flight deals. Some seasons are cheap to fly and stay in hotels. If you can't have it both ways (both sides of the trip), then it would still be available on one side and you can save some traveling money. Now let's look at some of the cheap days to fly:

For USA, Wednesday, Tuesday and Saturday are quite inexpensive. For international accommodations, weekdays are far affordable than the weekends.

Weekends are expensive, be it the US or other parts of the world.

You can take a red-eye and make the most of the available accommodations people are just too lazy to make. Everything will start to come in together once you get do it often and then more ideas will come automatically.

30. Deals on the Internet

"I want spam emails", said no one ever (I was holding that for a while). But if you are going for Asian trips, do look up the deals offered by their airliners and regional accommodations. Sometimes, even a friend can suggest a better idea because they have been there before. You can toy around with the ideas that you have and go for the one that serves you best. Those who dig deeper, do get the gold.

Chapter 3: Book a Deal Anytime on a Place to Stay

For people with itchy feet, traveling is a habit that dies hard. But when it comes to arranging your final travel plans there's one thing you have to have sorted out and that's your travel accommodation.

No matter where you go you will need a nice place to lay your head and get cleaned up. We are all familiar that the price you pay for a hotel room can vary greatly depending on when you book, the property and its location. You can cut down on the flight expenses remarkably well by choosing flight deals following the guidance in Chapter 2. However, if you are traveling on a budget, locating good lodging can be a daunting task but it doesn't have to be if you know where to look. The fact of the matter is that you can find affordable accommodations anytime, anywhere and land a deal at any time of the year.

All that is needed from you is to follow some simple steps to get the best prices. Just look for the right slots on the right places and you are sure to find something that is worth your while. Many people are doing it and there is no reason you cannot. Windows of opportunity abounds to save on accommodations. Here are some insider's tips to find the best deals around.

Collect Points and Stay for Free

It saves a pretty penny on accommodation costs that you can utilize in different activities. If you are not big on couch-surfing, this one is right up your alley.

It just takes a bit of vigilance on your part.

Whenever you stay in a hotel (this works for frequent travelers), make it a habit to collect hotel points via their programs and redeem them for free overnight stays. You can literally live for free. This is coming from a guy who lived in the Waldorf Astoria for free, courtesy of the points. Get the credit card offered by the hotel and earn bonus points. Put everything on the card and redeem them. So easy.

To earn points, you don't necessarily have to spend a ton of cash at the hotel – other methods are there, too.

So, next time if you are visiting a renowned city, chances are high that you can redeem your points and do much more, now that you have eliminated one significant expenditure.

Accommodation Resources that never disappoint

Listed below are some of the best websites for finding accommodation deals that are worth your while. Sporadic travelers and frequent travelers look at these websites to save a few dollars.

- Airbnb.com
- Priceline.com
- Couchsurfing.com
- TrustedHousesitters.com
- Agoda.com
- Booking.com
- Hostelworld.com

So, before you head out to some city, please make sure that you have looked over these options first. Do away with the hotel mindset! The world has become a global village and you should make the most of it. You have far cheaper and interesting options than ever before.

It will cut down the traveling expenses remarkably and free up funds for activities in the city. You can drink more, dine in more restaurants or even have fun doing the things that other tourists are doing.

All thanks to the internet, you have benefits that a generation of travelers never had, all things considered.

Priceline

This one has some benefits of its own. If you are visiting the US, this might be worthwhile for you. They have an option called 'name your price'. Let's get into this option for a bit. You look for accommodation in a city, think Miami for a while. Priceline will give you options in the category which would be more or less the same as offered by others. Then you input a price that you feel comfortable paying in the category (for a 4-star hotel, 3-star hotel or others). A lesser price may reveal more options which may not show up on the other search engines. It is time to put in the credit card information and hit the search option. If the website can find an option that you like, it will make the reservation for you and charge the credit card then and there.

Fun fact: Priceline has options that are so damningly cheap that they were unmatchable.

You will have to wait until Priceline decides to accept the offer you have in mind and your card is charged. You will get a discount on the standard price points, too.

This method is applicable to find hotels and lodgings anywhere in the world. Other than accommodations, you can also find rental cars and flights on the website.

Trivago

This <u>website</u> simply aggregates the hits it finds over the internet. It will search the hostel and hotel websites and gives bundles of listings. So, you can see everything that the competition is offering on one site rather than alternating between others in the category.

When you get the results, click on the hotels/hostels you are interested in. look at the benefits, options and specialties of the accommodation. Once you have decided on something, make a reservation over there and you are good to go. You can even pay in your own currency, if you like.

At Trivago, you can get some good deals so be sure to check it out during your browsing.

Hostelbookers

To find hostels if you like, you always have Hostelbookers. They as less listings when put in comparison to Hostelworld. But if you find one accommodation on both websites, Hostelworld will get the room for less. The difference might not amount to much, but during a trip, everything counts.

Say no to Hotels

Yes, you read that right. Hotels are struggling since the day Airbnb arrived. Coupled that with hostels and low-cost lodgings, they sure are under pressure in terms of declining market share. Airbnb offers great accommodations at prices which are less than the hotels. Interestingly, the prices of these apartments, houses and rooms do not change at all even at the last minute. The price of a booking is static. When you are done with the flight plan, Airbnb should be your next destination for accommodation.

If Airbnb fails, you still have Hostelz.com. It has around 45,000 listing in about 6,000 cities. The reviews from the travelers are great and you are in safe hands with it.

B&B is another terrific option for a last-minute and conventional route. The French hotel chain has a lot to offer and chances are you will find something here. Browse through its accommodations by date and place.

Input your email address to keep track of deals and promotional codes which are sent for your desired destinations.

Always remember: Heading to random inns may not work in your favor. Chances are that they can overcharge you for that. It happens everywhere.

Location-specific Booking

If you have a location in mind, look for site that offers low-cost deals in the area. For instance, CheapCaribbean is a platform that offers exclusive deals in the Caribbean region. Its last-minute section has listings on of both flights and hotel accommodations.

Another viable option is LastMinuteCruises is where you can find superb deals on cruises in Bahamas and Caribbean.

Also remember that not all websites will entertain the eleventh-hour tourist, so play it smartly.

Last-minute Deals

These are offered normally when the rates are dropped to sell a room. You can find tons of options on HotelTonight, which puts up all these deals for the customers. Expedia also offers its own last-minute deals section. But you should not overly rely on these deals. These are a backup, assuming that you do have a room with free cancelation.

Book in Hospitality Exchanges

A great idea to live in a different city for free (domestic and international) is to live in the house of a person that lives in that city. When you stay with a local, you have a range of benefits at your disposal. The local will give you information on the best places to visit, tourist traps to see, shopping options and also a tour guide, if you are lucky.

Many people prefer this option because it makes the trip a great cultural experience and you have friends for life. Some of the websites that can make this happen are given below:

- Couchsurfing
- Global Freeloaders
- Hospitality Club

Well, the first one (it is couch-surfing if you can't figure it out) is best of the best. It has the biggest and the most active community, too. The goal of the platform is to help form a bond with the travelers and locals in the area. You learn a lot about the local culture at the same time. Oh, also you save money.

The site has become a hot favorite for the travelers and backpackers alike.

It is understandable that people would be scared to take this option – a number of 'stranger danger' thoughts come to mind. You might think that they may steal your luggage and cash during nighttime or may murder you just for the heck of it.

Many of the people that do put accommodations online are former travelers themselves. They understand these risks better than you. Couch-surfing takes care of that and has steps which prevents these incidents. It has a thorough verification process and an option to post feedback and reviews.

A better criteria for picking a person is this:

Make sure that the person has a profile photo on the platform. It means that the person exists in real life.

The profile should be filled out completely. It means that they have invested time and energy in putting up the property online. If they find a half-filled profile, then simply move on. They are not invested in providing a safe environment for the tourists and you should not shortlist them either.

Check out their reviews. If a certain host has a glowing profile, that means he/she are popular among the travelers as the go-to option. You can feel safe because others feel the same. You may not like the person completely, but you will live with a peace of mind.

Look into their social media profiles. This is another huge plus point if they are active on their Facebook and Twitter accounts. It builds credibility and assurance that they are not hermits. Many people love social media and if you can find a host with an active profile, you are in luck.

Verify, verify and verify. The platform offers different verification levels of its own. People are verified by other backpackers and travelers. Apart from that, mailing address and credit card can be also verify their data. A verifiable profile makes sure that you are not leaving anything to chance.

Last but not the least, you need to use your own judgment as well. So far, the experiences on couch-surfing have been good overall. Sometimes, the host can be a bit anti-social or a jerk.

Talk to the potential host online and you could invite them for a call. This way, you can test the waters. Once you get comfortable doing it, it becomes easy and takes a load off your shoulders. Secondly, you will save thousands of dollars in accommodation costs and also have friend in every city.

Discount Deals from Booking.com

Well, trust me, you find this name coming up a lot as we go through this book. For those who don't know, Booking.com is the largest global provider of accommodation. When we say accommodation, it means everything. Guesthouses, resorts, hostels, hotels, camping sites, B&Bs and so much more!

It is fantastic for hotels and hostels. The prices are remarkably cheaper when you look at the competition in the market. You will find a ton of discount deals, especially in cities that are hotspots for tourists.

Another great feature about the website is that it allows the user to make a reservation without charging the credit card. Many times, a user cancels due to some reason and this amount is mostly non-refundable. You only pay on arrival.

Other than that, you can also cancel the reservation until 48 hours before the check-in. This is great if something else comes up and you have to take a rain check.

You can get rooms in any price point. Some hotels cost a few hundred bucks to a few thousand bucks a night. But you will find a room nevertheless.

The greatest benefit of Booking.com is that you can cancel bookings without incurring cost. As long as you follow the rules, you can work your way around nicely.

For novice and experienced travelers alike, it is a powerful tool. Some of the benefits of Booking.com are listed below:

- Prepayments are optional, not compulsory
- Professional and safe to access anywhere in the world
- Book without a credit card
- Manage booking in back-end as you need to

Newsletters, Newsletters and Newsletters

Well, it is one way to browse through a long list of listings, but you will find something that is worth your while. Bite the bullet, it will pay off.

Sign up for newsletters from AirBnb, Hostelworld and Booking.com and other leading names in the industry. This hack is also applicable to Vueling, RyanAir and other budget and high-end airlines.

Why should you sign up with the newsletters? You can always find an email, but you can never find random Twitter and Facebook posts that you saw by chance.

Yes, everyone has a barrage of emails to deal with, but this is the best way when you play it smartly. Also, when you feel that these emails no longer hold any value for you, you can just unsubscribe them. You don't have to see them for the rest of your life either.

So, once you get the hang of these offers and promo deals, you can keep an eye out for the ones that you like and negate the ones that are unviable.

Hostelworld and Promo Codes

For booking hostels, Hostelworld is rated number 1. They also have the largest assortment of camping sites, guesthouses and hotels and so much more. So, you can pick anything that strikes your fancy.

Not just that, they offer promo codes and run different contests, too. You can check out their website and be up to date on everything that they offer.

AirBnb and its Discounts

AirBnb is a giant and giving all the major hotel brands a run for their money. This option is the same as home exchanges where people can stay in rental spaces while they travel. The rental accommodations are immensely cheaper than the hotels and have more benefits in comparison. To spend a week or more, you can crash here if you like. Without investing a fortune, you get a comfy, homely space.

The apartments are amazing as something that isn't a hotel nor a hostel. For a solo traveler, you may have to cough up more cash, though. They are liable to cost nearly twice the amount charged by a hostel dorm room.

Airbnb is better-suited when you are traveling with a group and thus, per person cost dramatically drops down. This would take care of all the niceties that women want (not all women) and makes everyone a happy camper.

Lastly, you have your personal kitchen so you can do things on your own. Awesome, right?

People have been living in Airbnb accommodations for a while now. You meet new people, you get your own private space and it's squeaky clean. Everything is perfect about it.

Find a referral link from a friend or something, and you can get a $35 discount for your stays anywhere around the world. This is pretty amazing, right?

Steer Clear of Overbookings

For those who do not know the term overbooking, it happens when a service sells their beds/rooms even when they do not have the required capacity. This means that when tourists/travelers arrive at the hostel, they find that the hostel is booked completely. So, if a hostel sells 12 beds when they actually have 10, then the rest will sleep on the floor.

One way to avoid it is by booking a room/bed from the website directly. In this way, the reservation is booked 100% and no mistakes will be made when you arrive.

Incidentally, when the hostel that you required is out of accommodations, never opt for hostel that has a smaller size in comparison. Chances are that the availability has not been updated yet and you may be on the floor for the night. This can be avoided entirely by calling them up on their official number.

Avoid a Prepayment – Book via Phone or Email

Well, no accommodation would want to have this fun fact out there. It is bit of an insider secret. But this accommodation hack needs to be shared nevertheless. While booking with the reservation platform, or in other case, with the hostel websites, payment is made usually with the credit card. This deposit is non-refundable (now you know). So, if you do cancel it for any reason whatsoever, your prepayment is gone.

Side note: Some hostels do offer a free bus ride from the airport to the hotel and gives you the option to cancel 24 hours before your arrival. Different hostels offer different benefits.

Save money and book via phone or email! You would be surprised to know that many budget accommodations do offer this option and you can get a room this way.

Check out Booking.com and you can book a ton of hotels/hostels without having the need to pay upfront. Many hotels/hostels provide the convenience of booking an accommodation without a credit card.

For instance, <u>Hostelworld</u> has a few ways of reserving a room:

Non-flexible booking: The deposit is non-refundable if a traveler/tourist decides to cancel the booking for any reason.

Standard flexible booking: The deposit is safe and can be reused to make a different booking after a cancellation is made. This option has some extra charges attached.

Note: They now offer free of cost cancellations as well.

Important note: Everyone cancels a reservation at one point or another – happens to the best of us! Flight plan has changed or there is a change in plans, and so on.

Accommodations do not like to have their paid reservations cancelled. The rooms/beds are reserved for a duration and no one else can book it unless it becomes available. Last-minute cancellations can cause a huge dent in their profit margins. Truth be told, it is their safety net.

Book Hostels Well in Advance

It is interesting to note that the prices for hostel accommodations seldom change. The sooner you have booked your train, flight or donkey, book the hostel accommodation at the same time. Do make sure about the kind of hostel you want to have, and make plans likewise.

What is the reason to book in advance?

This is only because you have a much larger set of hostels to choose from. As is the case, the popular variety is gone before you know and you will be scraping bottom of the barrel yet again (god, I love this phrase).

In the case of 5 star hostels that are renowned all over the world, finding a spare bedroom or a bed for that matter is near-impossible. Some of these lavish accommodations even beat 5 star hotels, too.

So, never miss out on these hostels, no matter what you do. Be on time and it will be rewarding. You can quote me on that.

Travel Bloggers and Influencers get Perks

This is huge added bonus if you are either of the two. Luckily, if the target audience you have fits with the audience the hotel/hostel wishes to attract, then you are in luck!

The door to special deals and preferential treatment will open up. You can check their website and see how they are faring. Maybe, they need a blog post to ramp up popularity or maybe it is amiss from traveler's radar. You have to figure out the lapse they currently have and use it well.

If you are a photographer, you could show them your portfolio and bargain a deal. Same goes for the writing aspect. Every kind of publicity they can get for making a few compromises, is welcome for them.

Be realistic and show them what they can get, rather than showing what you have.

Pro-tip: People are always thinking about themselves and if you decide to go on and on about yourself, no one has time for that. 'Exposure' is a flashy term and chances are they would need more than a bunch of perceived benefits thrown at their face.

Also but: Take the goodies/freebies that the hostels/hotels offer you, but do not ask for them. Your Instagram must be marketable enough for that, or you are real famous.

Reach out to them and lay out what you can do for them!

Drop a bunch of hostels a tweet or a private message, whichever works. Throw some ideas and see what works for you and them. Then seal the deal and hop on a plane, pronto!

Accommodation against Social Promotion(s)

This is an extension of the previous section. For the masters of the social media platforms, they can make the most out of it. If you have a big following on Twitter, Instagram and Facebook, then you are in luck.

Get in touch with them and ask them what they are all about. You can fine-tune your sales pitch and think about what you can offer them. Then, they can see what you can bring to the table for them. It goes both ways, you give them something and they give you preferential treatment.

As a freebie, they could let you in some of the paid benefits. Drinks might be on the house or you could get some free lunches.

Now, let's talk turkey (business). As a social promoter and for people to take you seriously, you need to have these:

- Around or more than 5,000 Twitter followers
- More than 10,000 Instagram followers
- 1,500 fans on Facebook

These are conservative estimates and for bigger fishes, chances are you might need much more than these numbers. So, it is more a matter of what you have in mind and intend to focus on.

Note: This tip may not work with the high-end hotel brands that have a set audience. It works for those that are comparatively nondescript and require some pro-bono marketing arm of sorts. Your reach out to them would be futile and misdirected.

Book a Hostel and Choose a Partner Hostel

Okay, this may sound a bit confusing. It is a commonly known fact that many hostels are part of an existing hostel network. So, they can offer you a discount when you do book a hostel from their network. They will direct you to a partner hostel next time and also give you a discount. This way, you can almost get a room every time, in dire of circumstances.

Add-ons include free drinks or a 5 to 10 percent discount on their services. You end up saving more than living in a pricey hotel chain.

But this trick is not advisable in high-traffic seasons when these spaces are fully booked. In this case, preferential treatment goes out of the window.

Comparison Portals are Sublime

A comparison website is much better than individual checking the price points on multiple sites. These comparison sites cover a range of booking sites, and the price that you have depends on the particular site in question. So, it is advisable to look on the three major ones.

You can look for prices of the accommodations on the below-listed websites, though the prices change as per the season. Some have benefits over others, you can gauge which one works out best.

Kayak: You can set the 'price', 'amenities' and 'ambience' (this includes eco-friendly, family, trendy) filters on this website. It even has a freebies filter (parking, transportation, breakfast and luncheons).

TripAdvisor: A popular one in the niche, it gives vital information on hotel price, customer reviews and has some basic filters, too. But do look at the traveler ratings, which matters a lot.

Skyscanner: Known for mostly flight comparisons (the website, duh), Skyscanner can also compare hotels at the same time. You can use some standard filters to pick out a room that suits the time of your arrival. You can set filters for cancellation policy and meal plans, too.

Apart from these top three, your backup options are TravelSupermarket, HotelsCombined and Trivago to give a fuller scale of availability. Hotels.com also has a number of free stays, discounts and member-only prices, so be sure to check that out as well.

Now that you have done this, call the selected hotel and confirm these prices. Sometimes, they have something better and you could get an early booking promo or even a deal that is better than the one on the website.

Side note: Doing this has some pros and cons. contacting them directly would deprive of the loyalty points from the comparison sites. Direct contact may allow you to enjoy some freebies (Wi-Fi and drinks), and getting loyalty points from the hotel brand instead. This is something that requires a careful reflection. Choose wisely.

This tip has worked wonders for many of the frequent travelers and you can hop on the bandwagon, too.

While the option of hotels and hostels is ever-inviting, travelers are drawn to it because they experience the local flavor like never before. Some travelers also end up attending private parties, restaurants and sites that an ordinary tourist would clearly miss.

Chapter 4: Where to Find Last Minute Travel Bargains

Impulsive travel could be expensive if you play it unwisely. It is certainly doable to be spontaneous as good deals can show-up anywhere. You could be looking for last-minute hotels, cruises or even flights that will take you to a target destination. We will walk you through the steps to make sure that you make all the right moves.

For first-timers, selecting the 'right' time to travel may sound overwhelming as prices are moving up and down a lot. These fluctuations can be confusing when you have set a travel budget. But then again, you can work out the details when you have some expert guidance.

It all boils down to shortlisting a bunch of destinations and subscribing to the airfare alerts when possible. It will give you a bigger pool to toy with and you always need options to get a perspective of things.

In this chapter, we will guide you to best deals on last-minute flights, hotels, and cruises, because that is what we are here for, right?

Last-minute Airfare Deals

Airfare is in most cases, the single biggest expense in trips (domestically and internationally). The price tag depends on the supply and demand factor just the same. Price points are decided by a number of factors that include day of the week, time of the season and time of the flight alongside the destination.

Most of the airliners puts the ticket price on sale 10-11 months before the actual flight. But in this case, the customers are paying a premium price since the time slot from 6 to 11 months is expensive while the time slot from 22 to 121 days, the fares drop down considerably. In some cases, they are even at their historic lows, this is where the sweet spot lies.

In airline parlance, the last-minute period is from 3 weeks before a flight is set to take off. It is inadvisable to wait for more than 21 days for the prices to drop because that is unlikely to happen in any case. But if you are in overdrive, then it is better to look for competitive fares for any last-minute deals on Travelocity, Kayak, Expedia and CheapOair.

Once you shortlist a price, then be sure to crosscheck it through the airliner as well because in some cases, you may find a cheaper alternative.

Note: Always remember that inexpensive is relative. Budget airlines charge extra for everything additional. In some cases, they might cost more than the conventional legacy airlines.

Remember to be flexible with the airports. Large cities have incoming flights from many cities. For instance, you can reach Los Angeles from Burbank, Orange County or Ontario if it costs less than flying there directly. A short drive could save some dollars.

If you are in no hurry, then just set up an airfare alert. This will send an email when the ticket price of an airline drops that takes you to the desired destination. Google Flights, Skyscanner, Airfare Watchdog and FareCompare are ideal for these automated alerts.

You will find, like in the earlier chapter, similar flight-related information reiterated here but with an emphases on how to find great last minute bargains. When you book a flight before 48 hours of departure, you easily pay double the price for airfare. It is a necessary evil that you have to manage in crucial conditions.

Though, for all other cases, book flights when other passengers have a low-priority to fly – this puts you in a favorable position. Try to book flights in mid-week or the off-season when air traffic is remarkably lower. For the airliners, a low-price is better than a vacant seat and chances are you will find great seats at suitable prices. If you have time on your hands, then be sure to avail as many discounts as possible.

Book on a Tuesday or a Wednesday when the footfall in hotels are low and so is the case with airlines. When you book during the week, you will have a lot of options to choose. From favorite rooms to favorite flight seats, you have more room to work with. When you reach Friday, this is where you are at a disadvantage and the airline is at an advantage. In case of most roundtrips, you will find the best deals on the market when a Saturday night stay is involved.

Pro-tip: This advice is for the ones just starting out in the travel industry. Many of the airline websites list down last-minute deals on their websites. This is probably due to last-moment cancellations or other reasons. As a for-profit organization, every seat matters to an airline.

Follow Airlines on Social Media!

If all this downloading apps and frequenting websites isn't up your alley, then you can go for the next best thing. Follow the airlines on Twitter. Listed below are the Twitter handle of these airlines. Check them out and be on top of latest flight deals you might like:

- Alaska Airlines: @AlaskaAir
- Delta Air Lines: @Delta
- Frontier Airlines: @AmericanAir
- JetBlue Airways: @JetBlueCheeps
- United Airlines: @United
- Southwest Airlines: @SoughtwestAir
- American Airlines: @AmericanAir

Social Media for Everything

Just like the above point, you can harness the power of social media for just about everything. In this case, you can keep track of not just airlines, but also hotel brands and travel companies. Stay current on their sales, news and exclusive promotions.

Let's see some instances in this case:

Twitter: JetBlue and Virgin Atlantic routinely tweet their deals on their page. Apart from that, @TravelDeals allows you to see travel-related deals from many companies. It is fantastic how easy everything is with the internet.

Facebook: It serves the same purpose as Twitter. You can find tons of travel deals when you 'like' their pages. Though, it is advised to look them up only when needed because you get a barrage of needless promotional messages.

HotelTonight: The app bypasses contact with travel companies and offers a range of discounts. Though, it is also a great source for last-minute deals. It is a win-win for the hotels because they cannot afford empty rooms. So, they openly offer discounts of up to 60% on their standard pricing. Save those precious funds and you may dine out or enjoy that rollercoaster.

Booking Last-minute Cruises

Cruise deals are abundant over the internet. You can check out deals that are 3 months in the future, to cruise deals that are a few days ahead. Slightly dissimilar to airfare, the cruise prices start to drop as the date of sailing approaches. The staterooms on these ships sell out pretty early on, you can find other staterooms in comparatively less convenient or desirable areas. Now an embarkation may not be the best of places to have a stateroom!

If your residence is close to the seaport, then you can save a heck of a lot on the cruise trips and even take them more frequently.

Plan the last-minute trip to coincide with the incoming 'shoulder season' when sailing is dirt cheap. In the Caribbean side, the shoulder season is from September to November when hurricanes have a higher chance in comparison. December and January are the other shoulder seasons when holiday season is near.

The discounted cruises are abundantly found in Cruises.com, Cruise.com, Costco and Expedia as well. Also checkout Cruise Finder which can help get you onto the nearest boat on a whim. It gives you an overview of what's available across the US along with what deals you might catch along the way.

Last-minute Hotel Deals

Hotels can be quite within range if you book two days in advance. This may not be the case when a major event is planned in the city and rooms are pre-booked well in advance. Hotels.com is a lifesaver in this context. For any last-minute deals, you can use the platform, and it will never fail you. After the 10th night stay, it offers a free night stay, too. Most of the hotels have a habit to show their minimum rates on their home website, but Hotels.com is an all-in-one platform that can greatly save your time. Trivago and Room77 provide the same function and you can make a booking from their website.

Other than that, Priceline Express Deals is a bit different. It does not reveal the name of the hotel brand until the customers pay for it. However, once that is done, you can save around 60% from there on. Then again, if you are not a fan of any hotel brand yet, you can still find great deals for less money. You might save a few hundred bucks for the same hotel room that showed you a pricey room on its website.

HotelTonight has a ton of benefits. It will show you the room in advance that you plan to use during the trip. Quite a few well-known hotel chains are on their list and if that does not work for you, then go for the local ones in the city.

The app provides the facility of same-day reservations as well, which may work for last-minute travelers.

Then there is the points system, too. Though, if you intend to redeem your points, you need to book from the hotel directly. Some of the hotel chains are a bit generous and lets you pool points with friends/family if you need to live in a single room. The hotel staff can explain this one very well.

Tips to Find Last-minute Deals

This advice is probably for the occasional traveler, yet it will benefit them greatly. When planning a trip, you are at maximum advantage when you find deals in the following slots:

- Off-season
- When you don't have travel destination at all
- No need to fly

As said above, if you have no exact destination in mind, then you can find a bunch of deals from the weekly newsletters, cruise lines, hotels and even third-party booking sites. Chances are you will be toying with a bunch of options that seem suitable yet very appealing at the same time.

You can even find cruise deals on Costco Travel. The service provides you with Costco gift cards as well as onboard credits in addition to cut down prices. As an Executive Member, you also have the facility to get a 2% cashback bonus on any Costco Travel purchases. Besides that, you also collect reward points with their travel credit card.

Then again, do keep in mind the aspect of flexibility in getting last-minute deals and discounts. If you pick and choose any destination you like, it is more fun and you end up with a lifetime of experiences and ton of saved cash in your account.

Remember to Bundle up

Many of the airliner sites have an option to book an entire vacation package with them. This is something that Travelocity and Expedia have been doing for years on-end. You might stick with your preferred airliner to cash in the flight points and use it well later on. You can save significantly when you book it all (rental car, hotel, flight) in one place and there is the added advantage of it all confirmed in just one email.

If that is not the case, then TripIt will organize each and everything in one place.

Top-10 Apps for Last Minute Travel

For those having to fly urgently on a business trip, or a sudden plan shaped up to be a group thing, then you have a lot on your plate. First things first, find airfare and accommodation that suits you. You can download some of these reliable apps to get you started. Save money using these apps and all of them are free of cost on iOS and Android platforms, unless specified in particular.

<u>**Last Minute Travel**</u>

Its members can get a 65% discount on car rentals, flights, hotel rooms, trip packages and vacation homes. These members only pay a $50 annual fee. The app covers locations from all over the world. A sister app is also in works that is designed for boats and sightseeing tours.

One:Night

From this portal, you can book tons and tons of luxury properties in New York, Boston, Los Angeles, Miami, Washington and Austin. Starting from 3 pm, the users can select a hotel room for an evening and they can avail the bare minimum rate.

Trip.com

This app comes loaded. It has activities, dining and events, that you can look for based on the travel destination. You can save marginally on the standard hotel rooms (a discount of 25% is still a discount) compared to the published rates.

Expedia

It needs no introduction. For car rental, hotel room, flight or a complete trip package, Expedia is pretty easy to work with. It has gazillions last-minute choices for a tourist. Again, you can find discounts of 25% over here and in some cases, you can find discounts of around 50%.

Next Flight

It is a great app for frequent fliers. Yet, its up-to-date flight-related information is a godsend, especially when you need to hop on an airplane right away. You put in the essentials; origin and, destination alongside the departure data and see the magic happen right in front of you. The app will generate a list of flights available in your area and provides information on the arrival and departure times. Not just that, it will also give terminal and gate information so everything is taken care of.

On the downside, the app does not have a booking feature – it only shows the data that you need to take things forward. Though, you can call the airline and hotel to make the necessary arrangements.

Jetsetter

The slickly-designed app lets you do everything. From same-night stays in hotels to booking entire vacation trips, there is so much you can do.

Its feature, Jetsetter Now, has terrific discounts of up to 60% for its valued members.

In its section of curated tips, the editors go as far as to offer recommendations for luxury breaks, weekend trips and holiday tours that cater a certain audience. The app possesses a credit card scanning feature, which fills in the necessary details all by itself.

Its only downside is that it is available on the Apple platform for now.

Fun fact: The membership is free.

FlightBoard

It is a stylish app, inspired by the board at Charles de Gaulle Airport in France. It turns your device into a live board showing arrival and departure time of airliners. It info-dumps the flight schedules of 3,000 airports and updates information every 5 minutes. By doing so, you can see the real-time status of different flights.

This is app is great for any person in a rush to catch the next available plane and make it on time. So, if your city has more than one airports, it will display flight schedules of flights on other airports.

Momondo

Available on both Android and iOS, it is one of the most reliable flight-search apps out there. You need to find an impromptu vacation spot somewhere on the globe – no problem, this app has got you covered. Its Trip Finder section will give you a bunch of options to think about and finalize your plans.

The app has options on beach holidays, city breaks and also incorporates family-friendly settings. You can set a budget limit to see destinations that meet your needs. Time filters allows to see trips that are slated for the month or six months down the line. Set the trip you have in mind; fancy, social, romantic or just the cheapest.

Fun activity: Choose the 'anywhere in my budget' to check out flights, package deals and hotels that fall within a specific dollar amount.

Fareness

It is an app with a heart. This flight-search service shortlists the most inexpensive dates to fly for you from the internet. Conveniently available on both iOS and Android, it is better-suited for those who are flexible on the destination.

Although, you may select a desired location, go ahead and indulge yourself with South America, beach or even 'popular' and look through the options that grace your mobile screen.

Additionally, you can filter the trips by their lengths. You can go for a 2-day trip or a month-long trip for that matter. Apart from that, you can check out deals available for the next two weeks or coming months. This is where the app comes in handy again since you can work out price points that work out for you.

HotelTonight

The startup pioneered the concept of affordable accommodation at the last minute and for a moderate fee. The in-app platform lists down a nicely-curated hotel selection in 600 cities. The categories range from Luxe, Hip, Solid and Basic, facilitating quick decision-making.

You can book a room in under 10 seconds. The app has deals with these hotels, which is why they are able to move around the rooms like this. Now, they have an added feature which allows the customers to book a room for up to 100 days and the discounts on them are way better.

The geo-rate feature offers discounts to people based in particular locations. So, you might get a sweet deal if you are in your home city!

<u>Bonus app: Vrbo</u>

This app allows you to live in rental apartments and homes during travel. Just download the app and get cracking. Input the dates and travel destination and see the available options. The app even has a filter that gives you an option to 'book instantly'.

You don't need to talk to the property manager over the phone – the app takes care of that. Just a few taps and you have the place booked.

Remember a little research can go a long way so don't jump at the first deals that comes your way. You may be surprised on last minute travel discoveries as hotels, cruises and airlines can be very eager to get rid of rooms and seats that would otherwise go empty. Here are some additional thoughts for getting a sense of how to plan your trip in the cheapest way at the 11th hour.

Email Blasts are a Godsend

If you want an omelet, break the eggs. Many airlines and travel websites have their own weekly or bi-monthly newsletters. These newsletters provide information on hotels, cruises, flights and inside information.

All you have to do is check your inbox and you will find a treasure trove of discount deals.

Be Mindful of the 14-day Rule

When slots are empty, hotels, cruise ships and airlines offer discounts. This happens mostly when two weeks are left. So, it is advised to get your accommodation and flight schedule in order to avail a package deal. The more you are on top of things, the better for you.

Travel Agents can be Helpful

With so many options already listed here, people may forget about travel agents. Yes, they are still there. These professionals bring something else to the table, unavailable on the websites. They offer a personalized experience and can leverage their relationships in the travel industry, which could work in your favor. Some of the discount packages are disclosed to these professionals and your contact with them could benefit everyone.

You wouldn't know this, but the agents book with their travel suppliers. This means that they have access to exclusive deals you wouldn't find online. Additionally, they bring you their market insight and you could learn a thing or two from them (actually more than that).

Alternative Accommodations

These days, vacation rentals are becoming all the rage. Vrbo and Airbnb are some of the prominent names in the industry. As previously mentioned, these are private accommodations put up by the homeowners on these websites. So, chances are you will find great discounts over here and experience life as a local rather than a tourist. Interestingly enough, you can find these accommodations at a moment's notice and the price points are unchanged regardless of booking. Be it a week or a one day before, you will pay the same amount and have a room for sure.

You can find accommodations for groups or a single person with ease. This way, you save remarkably more and have more legroom at the same time.

Though, the vacation rental prices differ as much as their hotel counterparts, they are looking for minimum stays, so a weeklong vacation is simply not an option for them.

You don't have to live in Hilton Hotels & Resorts to have an amazing vacation. Once you select the city center or something of the sort, you won't be living in your hotel room anyway. You have to remember that.

Vacation rentals are also available post-Memorial Day. The further the date, the easier it is for the homeowners to offer their space or entertain requests.

Vrbo.com is an amazing option to pursue this option. You can even contact the realtors in this regard. A house on outskirts of the town is not half-bad.

Chapter 5: How to Travel for Free

Have you ever dreamed of one day seeing the world or reminiscence about visiting places you imagine growing up as a kid? Have you been longing to travel but really don't have the funds to manage it? Fortunately, today there are opportunities for you to fulfill that quest if you are industrious and somewhat adventurous. You will need to stay flexible and open-minded to travel largely for free. All it takes is a little planning and a well thought out travel strategy to get you on your way. Some of these options offer free transportation, others offer free accommodations; some require working, volunteering or utilizing your skills and a few offers them all or some combination. However, just like most things in life, all of the options come with their own tradeoffs and limitations, but if you're looking to travel for free or on a tiny budget, there're really hard to beat.

Crowdfund your Trip – Piece of Cake

Yes, it is possible now. You can fund your private trip from these crowdfunding websites. GoFundMe allows you to raise money from friends, family, and colleagues. They can even join you on this trip. How cool is that!

The catch is that if you fail to plan this 'volunteer trip' with sheer honesty, you are likely to lose longtime friends. Do make sure that the trip impacts the lives of underprivileged people. You should not take a trip in the guise of helping them while clearly, your intentions were far from that.

One fraudulent instance is that of a couple that arrived in Abu Dhabi to teach children. They came under false pretenses to teach children under 'some education ministry'. The news spread like wildfire and the faculty became well aware of their game plan. Whether they got away with it back home is unknown, though.

So, approach this platform with clear intentions. You have no idea how worse it can turn out for you.

Nursing Skills and Free Travel

As a practicing nurse, you can always visit Hawaii and Florida and get paid in return for your services. Use TravelNursing.org which offers you plenty of action across the country. From 8 weeks to 26 weeks, you can enjoy a change of scenery and some fresh air. Compensation depends on your skillset and experience. Some nurses can earn $1,000 a month and often their food and lodging are covered.

Go on an Educational Trip

Do you love kids and wish to take them out on and off on field trips or something? You would be surprised to know you can get paid for this now. Many educational travel outfits cover the expenses of a trip in return for your hosting capability. Some also offer boot camp before you head into the real thing. A few noteworthy outfits in the field are Explorica, CHA Educational Tours, and EF.

'Old Country' is calling

A handful of countries have this 'discover your roots' program for the expatriates to come back and enjoy for a wee bit. Some people do feel connected to their homeland and this program offers them a way out to return to their country. The programs are designed for youngsters so they can stay with the local families.

Some of the programs are listed below:

- Birthright Israel
- Heritage Greece
- ReConnect Hungary
- Birthright Macedonia
- Birthright Armenia
- CubaOne

Regardless of your heritage, research privately and publicly-funded programs to streamline your visit. Stay for free and take in the local flavor.

If you are serious about this option, do take some time to think about the citizenship program offered to the expatriates. For instance, Italy has a terrific program that offers dual citizenship to Italians (US and Italian). So, if you can prove that your ancestry is Italian, you can reap the rewards of living anywhere in the European Union. Isn't that swell!

Free-of-Charge Flying

This option is provided by budget airlines. You actually pay $0 for flights, if you keep your ears and eyes open. Okay, you still need to pay taxes, but you still win so much and lose so little. Be alert to notifications from airlines and pounce on them as soon as they drop. These offers are sort of flash offers.

A few airlines offer this convenience. Ryanair, EasyJet, Jetstar Airways, Virgin Australia, flymonarch, and Air Asia offer this sweet deal. Just sign up with your email and you are good to go.

Teach English as a Foreign Language (TEFL)

This might excite a lot of English instructors and for a good reason, too. If you have the TEFL certification (a course that certifies you to teach English to children), you are paid an amount that corresponds to the cost of living in the said location. The Far East and the Middle East regions offer have great salary packages, so you might want to target those. Sometimes, the accommodation is prepaid by the company.

Then, there is the option of conversational volunteering. English speakers can get rooms and board free of cost for the time they are in for conversational volunteering.

Diverbo has become a pretty popular option for youngsters. It's an intercultural and language exchange opportunity for native English speakers. A person who volunteers and is accepted into the program gets an all-expenses-paid holiday with full room and board for a week in return. There's just one catch, however, you just need to talk endlessly – that is required of you.

Vacation in Exchange for a Timeshare Presentation

This is the best bargain you can find if you stick to your guns. You have to sit through a timeshare presentation and you will earn a free of cost vacation. But this is a tough nut to crack – the salespeople behind these presentations are the best of the lot. They won't let you off so easily. You need to commit yourself to prevent a purchase.

The salespeople with their sheer weight of expertise entice customers into heavy purchases. It is almost a miracle if you can walk out of the room without spending a dime. Just think about it – why else would they throw so many free vacations if they did not have a high conversion rate?

Here is how it happens: A salesperson will deliver the initial presentation and quote. Some people will purchase at the initial offered price. Then, you get a one-on-one treatment where the salesperson drops the price a lot. This is where they tap into your vulnerability – people often give in and purchase their product.

They keep on going and drop the price remarkably low. The final price is a fraction of the initial price, an easy sell at that point.

Though people do take a lot of free vacations via timeshare presentations, but it is playing with fire. You could make an unlikely purchase that you will regret later on! If all this seems fine with you, then scope out the details here.

Timeshares are commonly seen in high-traffic vacation destinations. This includes Las Vegas, Walt Disney World, and different ski resorts. These are all pricey options and you may have to pay an arm and leg to avail their offerings.

Many companies use special promotions to entice buyers so that they sit through the presentations. This could range from a night stay at a famous destination or discount to popular tourist attractions.

Be a House Sitter

If you have previously done this before, then you are in business! You will be expected to take care of a house or some tame dog/cat while the occupants are off on a vacation. So, you have a new location to explore and a house to live in. How cool is that?

Now, it is even easier with companies like HouseCarers and Trusted Housesitters which connect people and travelers from all over the world.

Hostels and Work-Stay Accommodations

The hostels just like the organic farmers often find themselves in a sticky situation. With plenty of rooms and beds at their disposal, they offer free of cost accommodation and even free meals. In return, they expect you to work – some even pay a fee for your service.

It is not just the hostels with this facility. A lot of companies offer free of cost housing for short-term and long-term stay in return for work. Workaway and HelpStay are platforms that have eased this process compared to before.

Loyalty Programs are rewarding

Credit cards are not the only products that offer rewards. Hotel chains, airlines and travel entities offer loyalty points to travelers. If you prefer an airline, then you can rack up flyer miles very fast. The same holds true for notable hotel brands. Flash promotions are offered along with killer deals, allowing you to earn points rapidly and redeem them for flights or stays.

Travel blogs and travel forums are places where these promotional schemes are dropped from time to time. Here is a list of tips to travel at no cost with loyalty programs.

An Overbooked Flight is a Blessing

As a frequent traveler, you must have certainly experienced this once or twice. Every once in a while, some airline employee will announce on the intercom about an overbooked flight — They will offer an exchange – a voucher of $500 or something for any passenger to drop out of this flight and take the next one.

This option may not suit everyone. You may have an urgent meeting or a family emergency that needs your presence. But if you have no urgency to be anywhere, then you stand to save a lot more for losing a little.

In some cases, when the airlines have no takers, they raise the voucher's offering slowly. So, from $300, it could go up to $700, until someone gives in and decides to go for it. If the deal is worth your while, keep your eyes and ears open to grab it. You might have some competition. Here is how you can take advantage of these overbooked flights.

Swap Houses – So Easy

So, let's say that you live in Berlin and want to visit Seattle for a while. You can swap houses for the duration of that trip. Both parties win and you can stay in the house free of cost and enjoy the local flavor.

Meanwhile, your house remains safe from break-ins and other mishaps.

Okay – stranger danger is very real and there is no way going around this. You may not entirely feel convinced about a stranger living in your house for a length of time. He/she could steal stuff and deny it later on. But you are in luck. Many reputed home-swapping websites promise a certain amount of security, peer reviews, and identity verification, giving members some peace of mind. They also have credit systems to swap houses indirectly. When you offer the house, you accumulate points and you can redeem them later on for a pleasure trip.

Love Home Swap, HomeLink and HomeExchange are some popular house-swapping websites.

Note: Enter into an agreement with a clear mind.

Be a Travel Blogger

So far, most of the ideas mentioned above require something in return – so you can say that there are no free lunches. Trade of services do exist. So is the case with influencers and travel bloggers. Many travel bloggers get to travel free all-round the year. Incidentally, they may seem to travel on the surface, but a lot of work goes into what they do. As an influencer, you need to appeal to the business interests whom you aspire to approach. If you have a massive public audience, these interests will approach you themselves to pitch different ideas. This is when you are in business (pun intended).

Employment as an Au Pair

If you are fond of kids, then there are a lot of openings as an Au Pair (international nanny). This will get you a bunch of things – free board, free room, a paycheck, and some spending money.

A host family will keep you, so you can mix with the locals nicely. Some popular destinations to work as an international nanny include New Zealand, Spain, China, Italy, Switzerland, Sweden, Australia, and France.

GoOverseas is a platform that can make your dreams come true. Go ahead!

Sea for Free

Yes, you read it right. If the sea appeals to you, then plenty of opportunities are there on cruise ships and yachts. It is an amazing idea to explore the world. Work is hard, but opportunities are abundant. You can be a cleaner, chef, entertainer or so much more.

If you are interested in cruise ship jobs, then do check out carnival and Royal Caribbean websites. For yachts, you can try Crewseekers International, Find a Crew or crewseekers.net websites.

You do not necessarily need to have sailing skills. The crewmen just need some company, pair of hands and someone to take the watch and as such. You can even head down to the seaport and see what's out there for you.

Free Food!

Oh, boy. This gets better and better. While you travel anywhere in the world, you get free food along the way. Some people would be satisfied with that. If you are interested, then check out the Food is Free movement. It is an interesting concept.

The buzzwords here are Freeganism and dumpster diving. People in suits pick up food from the bin, which is hardly 5 – 10 minutes past its shelf life. So much food is wasted this way and this did not sit well with some people.

Gleaning is also a great alternative. The Falling Fruit website outlines information about trees in public vicinities that produce food.

So, if this sounds interesting, dive into the world of Freeganism and head over to Great Big Scary World. They have free food options in your area. Don't forget to check out the Falling Fruit world map on their website and see options that are worth your while.

Flight Attendants, Flight Attendants Everywhere!

You might know this already – but this begs repeating. These flight attendants are somewhat globetrotters at company's expense and get paid for it, too. Apart from salaries, they also get allowances and bonuses (depends on the airline). Discounts on leisure travel come as an added bonus.

You don't really need higher education, but at least you should have a GED. Here are some flight attendant jobs offered by airlines:

- Delta
- American Airlines
- Southwest
- United Airlines

WWOOF

It sounds like a funny acronym! It stands for World Wide Opportunities on Organic Farms. If the idea of living on a farm fascinates you, then this is your chance to make it happen.

Farming is just seasonal work and farmers need some extra hands when the season is on. So, keep in mind that they may not be the richest chaps you come across, though you can live, eat and have ample space at the farm. You may work 4 to 6 hours a day and have food and a room in return. Also, you will bear the cost of transportation as well.

Head over to the WWOOF website. Friends, solo and couples are all invited. Choose the country of your choice and the website will show you a listing of farms you can visit. The platform will connect you to the farmers as well.

Teach Abroad

A lot of teachers are roaming all over the world, thanks to their position as a visiting faculty. Round-trip flights are covered as is upscale accommodation with swimming pool, Jacuzzi, gym, and basement parking. Oh, if you are lucky, your income tax is exempt in some countries (such as UAE).

Some have it so good! They use the system to their advantage. For instance, veterans may do a stopover in Europe and enjoy the Christmas markets, food in Lyon and nightlife in Amsterdam. It is almost a dream come true.

Needless to say, you have thousands of international schools scattered all over the world. They require fluent English-speaking teachers, IT specialists, and admin staff. So, if this strikes your fancy, check out this resource.

Chapter 6: Students and Senior Travel Deals

You have a few months off for the summer. Trust me on this, you will never have this time again. No responsibilities and a worry-free mind are some things you will cherish later on in life. So, it is time to explore new possibilities and this break is the time to snatch your slot.

On the downside, you might be burdened with student loans, utility bills, and so much more. So, let's get creative and make the most of your options. Traveling should never be a distant dream.

Listed below are some viable deals and hacks that will let you travel cheap and allow you to stretch your dollar. So, start planning your summer vacations in a way you want and be ready to make some compromises. You wouldn't go far without it!

Discount on Flights for Students: The airlines in your country offer discounts for young travelers and students. You can book inexpensive flights as a student and reap the rewards that come along with it. Be sure to have promo codes to avail more discounts on the flights.

Also, check the airline alliance and airline policies, so you make your way carefully and cleverly to the desired destination. So, let's examine some of the programs in place by the leading American airlines:

American Airlines

Students can avail discounts offered on flights by the airline. Their AAdvantage scheme has special deals for the young students. However, you will need to show the student ID and fill in the relevant details to become eligible for the program.

Not just that, but you should also be on a student at any one university listed on the American airlines. If you have a group of 10 people or more, the airline is more than happy to give you a discount. You can reserve seats for as long as 11 months in advance.

Delta Air Lines

For booking international flights, Delta airline is a great option. These discount flights are also linked with Virgin Atlantic. You have more opportunities this way. Access more flights and explore more cities with this alliance. For instance, you can reach London from the U.S. and then head over to Manchester or Edinburgh. Choose from over 40 roundtrip flights between the U.S. and U.K. The alliance between Virgin Atlantic and Delta makes international travel very cheap and doable.

Not just that, you can even combine the Delta flights with Alitalia and Air France-KLM, which gives you a route to the largest transatlantic network in the world.

United Airlines

This is another airline that gives the students reliable and cheapest options for flights. Discounts are available on both international and domestic routes. Use the Skyscanner search tool to gauge the flight rates.

The GroupPlus program by the airline offers tickets for a group or more than 10 passengers. You can book these flights 11 months in advance. This is ample time for the students to save cash and finalize their plans for the trip.

The airline operates from 9 hubs — Houston, Denver, Chicago, Los Angeles, Guam, San Francisco, Tokyo, Washington, DC, and Newark.

Be it domestic or international flights, United Airlines gives the students an option to travel with a carefree mind.

StudentUniverse

Finally, the name that keeps coming in this chapter gets some space of its own. Their promo codes are quite popular among students looking for affordable flights. The promo codes offer discounts, albeit they come with strings attached.

If you come across a flight on StudentUniverse and STA, chances are that it belongs to some student-only flight deal. These two agencies are renowned for student discounts.

Skyscanner will also let you in a lot of affordable flights. In some cases, flights are cheaper than STA/StudentUniverse promo codes.

You will have to do some testing on this bit.

Southwest Airlines

The airline has discontinued its student fares, but the budget carrier still offers terrific value for money. The Southwest flights are ideal for domestic use. So, when the semester break arrives, you can always save your lunch money and head home. This way, it does not weigh on you financially and mentally.

So, compare various departure dates and find the deal that suits you at Spring Break and other vacation spots. Also, if you bring along a group of 10 people or more, the airline will waive the booking fees or some other cost.

As said before, it is terrific for domestic flights and does not hurt the pocket as much.

Lufthansa

The German carrier is a great option if you hope to touch more than one destination on your international flight plan. The airline has made a name for itself and known to very reliable. At discounted airfares, their airline offers 470 destinations worldwide for students from American colleges or universities.

The offered discounts are sometimes comparable or even cheaper than StudentUniverse and other outfits that offer discounted airfares to students.

Check out the prices at StudentUniverse first and use the promo codes, if possible. You can get an idea about how things are going in the market.

Accommodation Options for Students

For the students doing a spring break or something of the sort, you have to go with options that are easy on the pocket. The mission statement of Couchsurfing declares that it aspires to connect people from all over the world, enable educational and cultural exchanges and other noble stuff. So, you can always go for this option and save a pretty penny while you are at it. All it requires you to do is take a leap of faith. However, if all goes well, you can mix with local people and they can show you around the city. It will be fun and you get can firsthand knowledge of the people and their culture.

Student Discounts Cards

If you are a student studying abroad, then you should have the International Student Identity Card (ISIC). It packs a punch, offering discounts on public attractions to accommodations abroad.

It is accepted worldwide and gives you the status of a full-time student and access over 150,000 discounts across 130 countries. One piece of plastic has that much power! For non-students of 30 years and younger, they can get the International Youth Travel Card and take advantage of various deals.

Last but not least, the International Student Exchange Card (ISEC) is also something that you should have. It has travel discounts, discounts on cultural sites, B&Bs, hostels, museums and so much more.

Buses and Train Discounts

The student status gets you discounts in your homeland. Interestingly, the principle applies in other countries as well, especially for train and bus travel. For instance, students from 13 to 25 years have a 15% discount on traveling by an Amtrak train. In Canada, the discount is even better. Students can get a discount of 25% on Greyhound as long as they have an international Student Identity Card. A student ID card from post-secondary or American secondary school will also work just fine.

On the European front, Eurail comes to the rescue. While it offers discounts in different domains as well, you can get a discount of 35% if you are below 26 years old. That sounds wonderful!

Flight Discounts for Students

Student Universe and STA Travel makes travel less costly and so much easier. They offer terrific discounts for students on not just flights, tours, but also hotels, too. Some airlines have student discounts, too. Be sure to check those out.

Ridesharing

It is a great way to save money when two or more people are headed to the same destination. RdVouz is a service that connects riders with drivers on road trips worldwide. This makes it very easy to access new locations or travel like this. OpenRide and BlaBla Car are other options in the category.

Discounts and Travel Deals for Senior Citizens

Most of the discounts for senior citizens start from age 60 and above. Some of the businesses in the industry do offer them and they are scattered all over the globe. It includes rail, cruises, airlines, and others.

Discounts Offered by Airlines

The discount offered to senior citizens has fallen out of favor in recent times. Only a handful of airlines offer them for now. The most they can get is a 10% discount on the full fare of a normal flight. The age could range from 50 to 56 years. At first glance, a 10% knockoff may sound great, but with the rising airfare prices, you might be on square one. So, do check out airfare prices and use the elderly citizen card while you have the chance.

Some of the airlines mentioned below offer discounts. Check them out, you will find them useful:

American Airlines — the senior citizens discount is offered on domestic flights for ages 65 years and older. You can call American Airlines at 1-800-433-7300.

Air France — the senior fares are for passengers who are 60 years and older, but it is valid for just domestic flights. The proof of age needs to be shown and the tickets are refundable or changed in certain cases. You can call the airline at 1-800-237-2747.

British Airways — it has partnered with AARP and offers as much as $400 discounts on select flights, but only for the AARP members.

Delta — the airline offers senior discounts on some itineraries, however, they are not shown online. You will need to phone them at 1-800-221-1212.

Southwest Airlines — the discounts fares are for people over the age of 65 years and older. You will need to book it over the phone. Call 1-800-435-9792 for further details and limitations. Interestingly, the senior fares are refundable as well.

United Airlines — discounts for senior citizens are available in certain markets. Call the airlines at 1-800-241-6522 and confirm the discount availability for a certain flight.

You should also know that the regular fares of some airlines are better than discounted fares of other airlines. So, if some senior discount is not worth your while, you can opt for low-cost airfare. You can do this by following some tips and tricks:

- Sign up for travel and airline deals and newsletters on the internet
- Keep the dates flexible. For instance, savings are more on weekdays than on weekends. Secondly, a red-eye flight can save you some cash rather than taking a fully booked day flight.
- Check out the fees first. Airlines charge extra for stuff onboard. Things like food, checked baggage, and other things can cost you extra. So, travel light and keep essentials items only.
- Tickets for senior citizens are refundable and you can always cancel them. They may cost more than the special discounts offered by the airline, but it comes with added benefits. So, you still have more to benefit than to lose.
- If you cannot find the fine print of a certain ticket, call the airline and streamline details with them. You don't want any surprises.

Options for Rail

The discount on rail depends on your destination. Amtrak, for one, has a 10% discount for travelers 65 years and above. This offering is on coach class travel for senior travelers. The offer is available on nearly all the trains except Acela (a high-speed train), Saver Fares, Auto Train or any business class and sleeper accommodation units.

Over the years, Amtrak has kept its discounts for the senior citizens, it has vaguely specified the discounts to be discontinued. The railway company also has limited-time senior discounts from time to time. The present discounts include a 15% knockoff on San Joaquin, Pacific Surfliner and Capitol Corridor over the age of 62 and above. They even offer a 50% discount on Downeaster trains, which is pretty great.

For the senior citizens heading off to Europe, options are plentiful. As they say, having options in life is a blessing. No one railway line works for everyone, but it helps to have a few at your disposal.

Eurail Pass is pretty popular in Europe and offers the elder citizens over the age of 60 and above, a discount of 10%. Amazingly, Eurail is present in 31 nations and offers this discount in coach and first-class travel. Sounds swell! The catch is that the co-payments are quite high on all its high-speed trains so, you are still on square one, to be honest. Interestingly, high-speed trains are the ones tourists use mostly. The Eurail option is viable when you have to pass-through Europe for some days only.

So, if you need a lot of short trips, then a senior card is quite preferable. The card is valid for a year on all train tickets, which is pretty great. Some of the options, in this case, are listed:

- U.K. Senior Railcard offers a 33% discount
- French Advantage Senior card offers a 30% discount
- Italian Silver Card offers 15% to 25% discount (travel is free for people over 70 years)

Public Transit in Pittsburgh and Philadelphia

People over the age of 65 years can travel for free in both of these cities. This is an unbeatable deal for sure. Other than that, public transit systems in the United States charges the seniors half on commuting. The discounts apply on an all-day pass, multi-ride tickets, and single-ride tickets. Some offer perks on Medicare card or even a special senior ID. So, different systems have different benefits.

Grand Circle and Road Scholar

Started as Elderhostel originally, Road Scholar has unbeatable travel packages for the senior citizens. They offer tremendous value, continuing education, and great travel experience. To be eligible, you have to be 55 years and above. It is active in over 90 countries so you have a ton of options at your disposal. The tours with different options are on offer, from mild ones to tough ones. Road Scholar does great tours in the United States. The overseas tours are no less wonderful, be it the cruises or the tours. Though, the domestic ones are somewhat more wholesome. So, Road Scholar is terrific for anyone looking to expand their horizon or visit multiple countries.

For a conventional tour, there is always Grand Circle Travel, a company for travelers above 50 years. The tours are designed for seniors and offered in many countries. They stretch from the U.S. to Wales. It goes out of its way to cater to this age group, which is why it is so popular.

Ocean and River Cruises by Viking

Viking Cruises comes highly recommended by several people and critics. It is probably the best option out there. The company targets adults over 50 years and above for its cruises. The river cruises are generally more interesting to these people as opposed to Mexican, Caribbean, or Mediterranean cruises.

If your mind is set on an ocean cruise, Cruise Critic is another name that tops the list in the ocean cruise industry. Oceana, Silverseas, and Regent Seven Seas are its luxury cruises and you get your money's worth. It is on the expensive side though.

Also, Cruise Critic does not have the widely popular Royal Caribbean, Norwegian, and Carnival cruise lines, it compensates with Holland-America and Celebrity.

Rental Options for Seniors

You do not need to be a senior citizen to look for discounts on a rental cab. But when you go with the AARP deal available on Budget and Avis, you get a whopping discount of 30%. The base rate covers liability charges much better than anyone else. National is also a good option for seniors in this case. Their Emerald Aisle program allows the renter to select a car of their liking and use it. So, for elderly citizens who like to drive in certain cars, this option is pretty great.

Discounts on Accommodation of Seniors

In the case of most international hotel chains, discounts are modest and nothing fancy. They can range from 5% to 10% for seniors of various age groups (usually starts from 50 years and goes above). AARP offers some discounts and in some cases, membership is not needed. The deals of AARP are no less good than those offered by AAA and others in the industry. In the U.S. and Canada, senior citizen discounts are prevalent mostly. Independent hotels and local hotels do not have discounts in Europe and Asia, unfortunately.

Experience of people with AARP is mostly good and it is a good deal when others are not worth your while. So, do check out the rates on Priceline, Hotwire, hotel/airfare packages, and flash sales before you go for this last resort.

Chapter 7: Stress-Free Family Vacations and Travel

Summertime is just around the corner. It's high time to plan that family vacation you had in mind. The prospect of planning for a family trip can be stressful — with kids in tow, now you have more to figure out. You have to navigate your way through a cluster of hotels, flight seat selections, travel blogs, and activities for younglings.

So, we will first begin with a list of travel advice for families that will ease their planning phase. The hassle of planning can be hectic and traumatizing for some folks, so it is advised to keep a cool mind during this phase. Check out the list below for some basics:

No Google in the Start

As tempting as it may sound, Google is for a later stage of the planning. As a wholesome resource, it can create complete confusion. So, when you are just starting, begin by family meetings and identify everyone's wishes. Find out about the activities, how far they want to go and how adventurous they really are. Depending on their adventurous spirit, you could think of a country known for its beaches or another famous for its villages.

Looking at Google in the early stages opens up options that you hadn't entertained yet. Once you know the preferences of the family and ideal timings, you can plan out your vacation with ease and peace of mind.

Plan in Advance

School vacations and peak travel times go hand in hand. Planning well ahead prevents many disappointments. Some of these disappointments are mentioned below:

- Sold-out tours
- Insufficient seats on the flight
- Higher costs of travel

For young parents, the best time to travel is in January when prices are remarkably low. On the other hand, you can pay a pretty penny for traveling during the holiday week. With planning, you can send the essential items at the hotel room — many hotels accommodate this feature. This leaves space in your luggage for much-needed items. Travel experts recommend toys on board to keep the children occupied.

Ask Questions

It is important to streamline all the travel-related information to prevent any surprises. Ask about food allergies, sensory difficulties, and menu for allergic people in your family. This prior research pays off at the destination.

Talk to your travel agent or hotel management staff to work out all these fine details. They are well-informed and fully aware of travelers' issues. It is part of their job after all. Everything will be arranged well in advance.

For the independent planners, make a note in the local language and hand it over to them. They can read it and plan accordingly. The note should have all the food-related information for them to deal with you accordingly. Travelers with families should ask about strong scents in the hotel premises which could bother children/other members, so measures would be taken to accommodate them as well.

Realistic Expectations

It is unrealistic to plan out several activities. Though, it is realistic to plan out select activities and accommodate 'travel' and 'wait' times. Many families head over to a destination with so much in mind, yet do a lot less once they arrive. They fail to factor in rest time and make smart moves that allow them to make the most of their time.

The famous hotel brands can also give great directions on the activities that are the most fun. It would be honest and firsthand advice. So, keep your schedule flexible and manage activities in order of their priority.

Secondly, the flights can be boring at times. So, talk to the kids and make their flight interesting. Get them all excited about the trip. Don't forget to keep toys for the flight. Children are bored very easily inside closed spaces.

Pro-tip: Keep the blue painter's tape, it keeps the children occupied. It is easy to get and available everywhere.

Most importantly, take photos of theme parks and other spots. If your children wander off somewhere, or you take a detour which leads to an unfamiliar location, people can guide you from that photo. It is an interesting hack and works like a charm. Ask the employees or locals and they will surely help gladly.

Lastly, check the expiration date of passports. Children have 5-year validity while adults have 10-year validity. Be sure to check them in advance, otherwise, you may have to cancel the trip.

Vacations should be Fun

Yes, the planning phase is stressful and traumatizing, but it is worth it. So, when all is done and dusted, you can simply reach the vacation spot with peace of mind and look forward to all the planned activities. Vacations are all about getting your mind off routine matters and give it some space.

Most importantly, if you think a certain vacation spot comes with added difficulties, it is better to look for an alternate destination. When you are ready to take the big trips, you will do them. There is plenty of time in the future for that.

Top-10 Family Vacation Spots in America

If you are a European reading this book, chances are you need to narrow down some spots for a quick getaway or two. This section has scoured spots from all over America and found destinations that are a must-visit. So, pack up your bags because you are in for a blast. Wilderness, beaches, and high-adventure await you.

Hilton Waikoloa Village

Located in Hawaii, the renowned Hilton Waikoloa Village offers endless beauty, things to do and luxury. For parents looking for child-friendly activities, book a spot in Club Keiki. Children can feed swans, look for treasure and have fun with tide pools.

Hudson Valley, New York

Only 50 miles away from main New York City, Orange County forms one portion of the vast Hudson Valley in New York. The LEGOLAND New York Resort is also slated to open in this area on July 4, 2020.

It will be the biggest park of its kind, consisting of 50 rides, attractions, and other unique offerings. The LEGO Factory Adventure ride will provide a replica of the person on the ride, which adds to the overall fun. It is going to be a tiresome day at the park for sure.

Park City, UT

It is a renowned snowboarding and skiing destination and boasts of the largest lift-accessible ski terrain in America. Children and beginners can take lessons at Park City Mountain's High Meadow Park. You can learn about wide-open and gentle slopes over here. It is perfect for beginners.

The lovely Woodward Park City has both indoor-outdoor sports and a ski resort. It has the longest snow tubing lane, many trails for people with different levels of experience, BMX, scooter, and skateboarding options as well.

Get a taste of actual winter sports at Utah Olympic Park, originally developed for the 2002 Olympic Winter Games. The family can tour the 400-acre venue and view a range of sites. The Nordic ski jumps are a great sight. The Discovery Zone has climbing structures and a playground for children. The adolescents can try their hand at ropes courses and ziplining, too.

Apart from that, Park City has tons of activities, too. Biking, hiking, and other fun-filled activities are available in other seasons as well.

San Diego, California

Visit the sunny side of California. San Diego has a bunch of fun-filled activities. It has water parks, theme parks, kid-friendly museums, and a coastline that stretches for 70 miles. Use the Go San Diego Card and get discounts at Balboa Park, Legoland California, San Diego Zoo, harbor cruises and museums for that matter.

Bar Harbor, Maine

The small town in Maine offers swimming at Echo Lake. It is a freshwater beach and very safe for children. The town has trails for cycling, walking and even hiking. Signposts on the streets will direct you to the 'Museum in the Streets'. Finally, Acadia National Park boasts of beautiful coastline views, and options for hiking and camping.

If you are in the area from July 17 to August 21, enjoy free popcorn and family-friendly movies at Agamont Park.

Winter Park, Colorado

For many, Winter Park is a winter destination. A little known fact is that it is also a summer destination. For the summer crowd, summer discounts are available at the famous Winter Park Resort. You can do horseback riding, biking, hiking, zip-lining, rafting, and enjoy the longest alpine slide in Colorado.

Snow Mountain Ranch is nearby. It has the only summer tubing hills in the whole of the USA. You can also enjoy swimming, miniature golf, and outdoor climbing walls.

Grand Canyon, Arizona

This natural park has over 2 billion years of geological history.

The Grand Canyon is the most distinguishable landmark of Arizona. The natural wonder stretches 277 miles from one end to the other. Everyone should experience this nature's wonder once in their life. The park celebrated its centennial anniversary in 2019.

You can find mountain lions, condors, elk, and 1,000 plant variations that have thrived in this semi-arid desert to this day.

Glacier National Park, Montana

Head to the Big Sky Country and get a load of hiking, dog sledding, skiing, and whitewater rafting. Opened to the public a century ago (in 1910), the national park occupies one million acres. It has serene and beautiful landscapes. Just to give you an idea here, the national park has:

- 762 lakes
- 175 mountains
- 563 streams
- 200 waterfalls
- 25 glaciers
- 745 miles of hiking trails

Disney California Adventure

The Californian Disneyland is rated as the third-best park in the world, right behind DisneySea and the first Disneyland. The Buena Vista Street brought tremendous attention to the theme park while Cars Land gets a lot of attention as well. Kids can enjoy so many of the rides. The popular ones are:

- Toy Story Midway Mania
- Luigi's Flying Tires
- Radiator Springs Racers

Disney World Florida

The magical kingdom of Disney was opened to the public in 1971. Today, it is one of the most-visited theme parks in the world. With the Cinderella Castle as the centerpiece, the park has rollercoasters, rides, and attractions spread over a 107-acre area. The magical kingdom is located in downtown Orlando.

Top-6 Holiday Destinations in Europe

For the families with Europe in mind, this list sorts out everything for them. It's a vacation after all and for many, the crowded cities are just not their thing. This opens up a broad range of options for you. From

Barcelona, Greece, to Romania, you can dive headfirst into European natural beauty and picturesque landscape.

Algarve, Portugal

It is one of the most wonderful regions in Portugal with weather that is mild and sunny all-year-round. Algarve is a treat for the sore eyes and you should definitely visit it with your children. Its golden beaches, blue waters, and Benagil caves are to die for!

Algarve has all kinds of accommodations. Be it villas, guesthouses, hotels, or apartments, you can find them all here. Watch the dolphins in Algarve, one of the best spots to watch dolphins in Europe. After that, take a Jeep safari tour and enjoy nature up close. It is going to be a blast.

Barcelona, Spain

Barcelona is a treasure trove when it comes to family adventure and sightseeing. It is exceptional for families. Start with Sagrada Familia church and PortAventura theme park first.

There is a lot to do in one of the busiest and beautiful Spanish cities. Head over here or <u>accommodation options</u> in Barcelona. Something will be definitely right up your alley.

Provenance

Orpierre is a medieval village in the Hautes-Alpes department of Provenance. The area is a rock-climbers' paradise. For the experts, Belleric, Quiquillon, and Adrech are there, while the newbies can head over to Quatre Heures cliff.

If that sounds a lot of work, then the inflatable climbing tower and the climbing walls at Camping des Prince d'Orange are your last resort. The area has a huge campsite with posh tents, mobile homes, and facilities, which provide convenience to families. From the swimming pool, mini-golf, biking, and film room, there is a lot to do.

Austria

Austria is less renowned in the family vacation category. It has no less shortage of vacation spots and activities for children, though. Chasing chickens and lamb-petting are just for warm-up.

Spend a few days in wooden chalets and visit the family-friendly farms. The stench of cow dung and dry hay is so tempting for the urbanites. Bauernhof Zieplhof has a picture-perfect view of ski slopes. Let the children try pony riding, they are only going to get better at it.

Romania

Suitable for children above 14 years, Romania is a fun-filled adventurous ride for the children. Take mountain-biking trip in the Carpathians, the remote villages in the area have good enough accommodation to crash for the night. The single-lane tracks are great for riding your bicycles. Your trip will start in Bucharest, taking you through strange hills and beautiful woodlands, passing through Dracula's Castle in Bran. The difficulty level is medium and it is 37-km of pure adventure.

Mountain hut, Switzerland

Trekking a mountain to stay the night in a remote spot is nothing short of adventurous. A weeklong stay in the mountain is truly refreshing.

The view of wooden cabins, the bleat of goats and 'mountains on fire' at sunset are spellbinding sights.

The Swiss tourist board has even facilitated an Airbnb of mountain huts, provided on the website alp.holidaybooking.ch., it is another one of the best vacations you will ever have in your lifetime.

Greece

Good for children of age 3 years and above, a trip to Greece is memorable. They will cherish the trip for years to come. The famous Pelion peninsula which is 60-mile long has its charm and history. Visit the whitewashed villages near the peninsula and purchase crafts. You can also find museums, Byzantine churches in Volos, a hill village in Milies, and well-preserved mansions.

With its infinity pool and self-catering villa, it is ideal for a weeklong getaway, far from the madding crowd.

Must-download Mobile Apps for Family Vacations

Planning a family vacation requires working out countless things, so be ready for that — don't be fussy about it and never skip details because it's too much work. Luckily, a lot of apps will make vacation planning quite easy. Apple and Android stores are cluttered with travel apps so there is no dearth of travel-related apps. But we need the best of the lot. Listed below are some apps that are highly useful for family and non-family travelers. Although it's a vacation and all, you are not leaving your house without smartphones and handheld devices. Enjoy some time with the kids without any technology — but do not forget to consult it — apps will make your life easy by comparing parking prices, navigating traffic, finding restrooms, and so much more.

Yuggler

Available on iOS, Android and 99 cents, this app allows you to find nearby attractions — worth-it attractions and free events both. You can Yuggler to find activities and decide based on the weather and mood of your kids. Check the reviews left by the parents and decide the best one for the day. You can save hefty entrance fees by opting for free events. Just download the app and let the fun begin!

My Disney Experience

It uses the interactive map of the Walt Disney World app, allowing you to find nearby attractions, restrooms, and restaurants with ease. You can also check out wait times for popular rides and plan your activities while you are at it. Even though it does not have any discounts for its users, but it saves the parents so much time and keeps them sane! If your children are small, we would suggest you download the app before the trip.

Sit or Squat

It's the perfect app to find the public restrooms nearest to you. One function that is actually the most important is the audience's cleanliness score. You will never have to enter a coffee shop for that unnecessary cup of Cappuccino with this app ever again. It's free to download and also available on iOS and Android platforms.

Postagram

Do you miss your grandma/grandpa during the trip? Now you can send them postal mail very easily and via an app! That's right. Postagram turns the snaps into postcards (with an in-built function). Just upload the image, type a quick message, and place the order. The app prints the postcard and sends it anywhere in American for just $1. So, keep your grandma/grandpa posted with travel photos — as many as you like.

It's free to download and also available on iOS and Android platforms.

Wi-Fi Finder

Now you can find a Wi-Fi spot nearest to you. The Wi-Fi Finder app is just for this purpose. So, before you step out of your home, download the offline database on your phone so you can save some mobile data looking for a hotspot — much-needed during an international trip.

The app is available on both [iOS](iOS) and Android platforms.

OpenTable

As the name implies, it's a table-reservation app. For every meal, you will earn some points. One table reservation earns you 100 points while other spots can earn you 1,000 points — every 100 points is $1 earned.

You will receive a gift card by OpenTable to save you some money on the food.

You can search the restaurants by applying filters — price, cuisine, and distance to pick a spot everyone likes. You can also read the audience reviews on the app to gauge other factors (noise level, friendly for kids, and other stuff).

The app is available on both iOS and Android platforms.

TripAdvisor

This app comes highly recommended. The app suggests points of interest, activities to do, hotels, and so much more. You can develop a customized itinerary for a family vacation. You can even access this itinerary and other tour-related information on your phone for offline access.

Lyft and Uber

Ride-sharing can be quite useful during your family getaways. The car rental and taxis can put a huge dent on your budget but Uber and Lyft save you from that.

Always use these apps and decide the better of the two (based on wait time, travel charges, and other stuff).

Lyft and Uber can work for families of all sorts, especially the ones with grown-up kids — it might be a bit dicey for younger kids.

Note — you would be surprised to know that taxis rip the tourists in international destinations all the time.

Snapseed

It's a great photo-editing tool. So, if want some bragging rights to go along with your trip, then Snapseed is it! You can edit your photos and beautify them with ease. Post it on Facebook, Instagram, or wherever you do it. The editing tools of Snapseed are for both beginner and professional photographers.

TripIt

On any average family vacation, you have a flight and hotel room to book, get a rental car, reserve a table in the restaurant, and explore the city for activities.

TripIt will take care of all that easily. It will track these moving pieces and keep your mind at ease. Just forward the details to an email address and the app works out everything and shoots you an email. Viola!

USA Rest Stops

Just download this app and you will never need to look for gas stations on major highways in US states anymore. With this app, you can check out the proximity of a rest stop and how busy it is. Activate the app before leaving the house so you are covered on this end.

The app is available on both iOS and Android platforms.

HopStop

If you are a solo traveler or with a group of friends, public transportation is a boon, really. Just download this app and check out the schedules of trains, subways, and buses. It also relays the costs of all three so you can pick the one you like.

You can download this app for free from the iOS platform — it is free to use in over 600 cities across Australia, Asia, Europe, and North America.

Waze

Now you are on a clock and traffic jams are the last thing that you have planned for. Fret not! Just download this free traffic navigation app and get great driving directions — whether you are in a rental car or on the driving seat. It re-routes you around the traffic jams in the area, guiding you by voice through various turns, signals, and stops. It can also estimate the time of your arrival, nearest gas station, and other important stuff.

The app is free to download on Windows, iOS, and Android smartphones.

PackPoint Packing List

It's your travel companion. While packing for a vacation, the current weather conditions could completely slip your mind. Fret not!

This app gives suggestions on packing, based on the number of days, planned activities, and weather in the area. The app has many more facilities that you can come in handy for you.

It app is free to download on both iOS and Android smartphones.

Amazon Prime App

Okay, it's not what it looks like — it's not a streaming app. Amazon Prime app is a great app for ordering household supplies and groceries off the internet. It delivers in major world cities right to your doorstep in a few hours.

The pricing is competitive — you will have to pay extra for a 1-hour delivery or give a tip to the delivery guy. Now Amazon Prime Now even delivers take-outs from restaurants. You can order restaurant food and grocery supplies right from the app, making your life so easy. The room service fees can be a lot when you are on a trip so you can save precious travel dollars this way.

Parking Panda

As the name implies, it resolves your parking issue. Rather than circling the block — again and again — you can find a spot now with ease. It will list garages with available space, reserve a space, and pay via the app as well. The app works in over 40 Canadian and American cities (major cities always have parking problems, obviously).

Trekaroo

Call it TripAdvisor for families. The app has helpful reviews of family-friendly spots in Canada and the USA. Not just that, it also has tips from travelers and gear recommendations for children. Select any state and find out the hotels and highly recommended family-friendly attractions. You can also set the filter for low-cost and free attractions.

Western Spirit Cycling Adventures

If you are an avid cyclist, then this is your true calling. Explore the country on two wheels with the family in tow. Western Spirit has guided tours of national parks, monuments, and even Black Hills National Forest. You can avail a 30% discount on budget travel deals offered to the customers.

Find Your Park

For the lovers of national parks, this is 'the app'. An app from National Park Service, it offers a plethora of options for you to finalize the next park excursion. Parks usually have low entrance fees and much more to explore, so you have a lot to do in a day.

Family Vacation Critic

This [website](#) has plenty of ideas for family vacations! Browse through the specific articles on the website to find the next vacation site. It could be African Safari, a top-10 list of national parks in America, or check out resorts that offer a range of activities for you and the kids. It also has tips, hacks, best time to head over to a location.

Google Flights

It has become a popular way to search for airline tickets. Google Flights crunches vast data to bring you the most convenient dates, times, alternate cities for you to select and choose from. The app is neat, organized, and easy to work with. Its money-saving maps are a vital feature as well.

Tracks and Trails

If driving an RV in a national park is your idea of an adventure, then this app is it! This app will prepare a personalized trip for you and your family — from renting, rock climbing, avoiding tourist traps and so much more — you have nothing to nothing about. You can save travel money by heading in the offseason when footfall is less — April, October, September, and May — and enjoy the calmness of the natural surroundings. You have more sweet deals during the offseason because business must go on and deals are unleashed for tourists in this season! You can also save in RV costs because those same RVs cost a lot more during peak season. Be sure to visit the Rocky Mountains in their most-preferred excursions of the lot.

City Maps 2 Go

People do not carry those heavy guidebooks and maps anymore — they now rely on virtual maps on their phones. But what if you are in a remote location with no mobile coverage? Google Maps are not reliable all the time. So, before you head over to a city with poor receptivity or connection issues, use this app-based map to download offline maps and find your way through easily.

AwardWallet

This app is for frequent travelers. So, being a frequent flyer, you need to be a member of travel loyalty programs — hotel points, flyer miles, and other stuff. You can track all this with AwardWallet now. The app will save your membership login information for all the active programs. So, make the most of this app and your accumulated points.

Dosh

Everyone wants their cash back and now so can you! Download this app and get some of that cash in your account. Dine out, visit the local attractions, and book your hotel rooms and save at the same time. Link the credit card and cash are rewarded when you make payment. You do not need to track anything — which you are already doing so much during the vacations.

Amazingly, hotels are available at a lower price than on the major hotel booking sites — so save some money here. The app sends more cash your way when you complete your stay in the hotel. This is the best app to save cash and earn some on last-minute vacations and trips. You cannot find anything better than this for now!

Undercover Tourist

You sure can save money at Disney World now. Undercover Tourist is as real as it gets. The authorized seller can save you up to 30% of costs on hotels, Universal Studios Orlando, SeaWorld Orlando, and other attractions. You can get information on the best times to visit, waiting times, line-length estimates, and show schedules.

ATM Hunter

It's a free app from MasterCard which helps you locate the closest machine in the area. It will use the GPS to find an ATM and points you in that direction. It can do both — find a bank or an ATM in the area.

The app also works internationally and relays much more information — which may or maybe not of interest to you.

The app is available on both [iOS](iOS) and Android platforms.

Gogobot

It is a travel-planning site but now is also an app. It has tips from many travelers. The app is divided into 19 tribes. You can join the 'family' tribe to check out the reviews, ask questions, and exchange tips on the platforms. Handy guides are already there, saving you from asking people questions.

Chimani

This app has details on 400+ units under the U.S. National Park Service — you have open access to information on seashores, historic sites, national parks, monuments, and much more. The app has thousands of images of national parks and other natural spots. You can collect badges and earn points as you visit each park.

The app provides general park information, a schedule of shuttles, scenic views, waterfalls, food and lodgings — and of course — the nearest bathroom as well.

The hiking section in this app steals the show! It features 27 hiking trails with map locations and write-ups for your convenience. The hiking trail details are also given — elevation, length, the time it takes to finish a trail, difficulty level, and other related information. So, it has a trail for everyone.

For your information, the app has standalone apps for individual parks as well — these are also free to download. Additional information links are also given in-app. The app needs an internet connection to download all the data, but you can later use it offline with ease.

MyTSA

With this app, you can cross-check the weather conditions, carry-on rules, flight delays, and so much more! The app from the Transportation Security Administration helps families move through security easily. Passengers are also given an option to post their feedback.

The app is free to download on iOS and Android platforms.

KIDzOUT

This is app pretty convenient for all the young parents out there! You can find the nearest diaper changing station, family-friendly restaurants with play area available, and more. The app uses the GPS function to look for attractions in your area and provides dining options with the kids' menu. It will also let you know about medical facilities nearby to deal with an urgent situation.

The app is free to download from iOS and Android platforms.

XE Currency

It's a currency conversion app. You can determine the price of any commodity with this app. Set your base currency and calculate rates from USD and other currencies — this will let you decide the importance of those commodities.

The app is free to download and available on Windows, iOS, and Android phones.

Chapter 8: Going Alone – How to Travel Solo and Get the Most Out of Your Trip

Traveling solo can be a liberating and empowering experience like none other. It allows you to connect and enjoy a destination on your own terms-without the distraction or schedule of others. No matter what your age group, traveling alone provides an opportunity to become more self–aware and help puts life into perspective. Even for first-timers, solo travel is like a religious experience. It is wholesome, unbiased, unfiltered and free of diverting thoughts of a fellow traveler. Solo travel is ideal for a full-scale indulgence.

Everyone needs to travel alone at once in their lifetime. Yes, there are challenges and some risks to consider. Frauds and dodgy salesmen are common while customs and traditions and everything in between are new. So, it is advisable to reach out to fellow travelers who have prior experience of the city and initiate a Q/A session with them. They will most likely save you from some preventable mistakes. Some heads up is always nice.

Some issues are timeless in solo travel. These include loneliness, safety concerns, and that 'single supplement'. But don't worry. Some common sense and prep will save you from additional trouble. It sure is a liberating experience and you gain more inner confidence.

The biggest benefits are traveling on your own terms and taking decisions without any undue influence. Listed below are some common travel tips for first-timers. Read them and you can save yourself from some unneeded trouble.

Say no to Single Supplement

Many hotels and cruise lines offer single supplement options. However, they have to make up for their losses, so, understandably, they charge the same for one person. If that is the case, prefer to share a room with another fellow traveler and save a few bucks. They will be used up somewhere else.

Do remember to ask the price so you can compare the pricing of different providers.

Find an Accommodation with Stellar Rating

Solo travel can make you vulnerable sometimes. Only find accommodation options that have multiple positive ratings and roaring feedback from the audience. Airbnb is great in this regard and read the above chapters for detail on those. The reviews will make a few things clear about the property — type of neighborhood, kind of host who lives there, if more tenants are sharing the space right now.

Keep a Camera Extender/Tripod Stand

Yes, you will need this at times. Traveling alone should not limit you at all. Some equipment makes the journey feel more satisfying and complete. You can take all the prime Facebook snaps right in front of famous tourist spots.

You never know when a stranger may run away with your camera/DSLR, especially when it is pretty expensive. It may have taken you months to buy that, but only a minute for a thief to get it.

GorillaPod has excellent mounts for DSLR and handheld phones. Do check it out!

Some Lightreads

Since you have a two-way flight, many nights in the hotel room along with commuting, a book or two would fit in nicely. This could be a great time to take up those books that were lying on your table, gathering dust.

Books are nice companions and take your mind off the mundane stuff. Secondly, if you are an avid reader, then these slots would give you the much-needed time to get back to your reading and maintain your speed on yearly challenges.

Visit coffee shops. They also have a book collection mostly. Strike a conversation with a fellow reader and you might have a travel companion. Make sure that books do not compromise your luggage space. Play it smartly.

Send the Travel Itinerary to Everyone

This needs to be done as soon as possible. Firstly, make an itinerary and send it to friends and family. It should have hotel reservations, flight timings and everything in between. Be sure to send daily updates to everyone so that people know about your whereabouts. Register yourself at the State Department. This way, the local embassy can contact you anytime when needed.

Emergency Contact Information

Again, this is very important. Keep emergency contact information at the ready and make a few photocopies of it. This list should have names and numbers of all the family members and close friends. These measures will ensure that if your luggage mistakenly exchanges with another one, you can get it back easily. Some people may contact you, while some may not. It depends on your luck.

Secondly, if your credit card is stolen, you can contact the company to block it immediately. They will activate the travel protection benefits.

Free Wi-Fi is a Must

You need to keep in mind the timings at which the city tends to get dark. It varies, suffice to say. So, if you are not much of a fan in nighttime exploration, then you might be staying at the hotel for quite some time. So, make sure to book accommodation that has free Wi-Fi. This way, you can post pictures every day and use the time for relaxation and connecting with people.

If Wi-Fi comes at an added cost, you can drop that lodging and find one that does offer free Wi-Fi. Other than that, use the American

Express Platinum card to gain access to Wi-Fi hotspots anywhere in the world. Check out the <u>Boingo</u> website to see the availability of Wi-Fi.

Start the Day Early

If you have done bar-hopping quite a lot by this age, you can do more productive things in a foreign country. Be an early bird and make the most of your time. You can visit popular tourist attractions when the crowds are still deep asleep. Bustling cities stops for none and you should definitely understand that as a tourist.

Leave Comfort Zone Behind

When you are traveling solo, you can do so much more on your own. You are not at the mercy of friends/family. So, this is a great chance to try out something that you wouldn't do with a group.

For instance, you can head over to some art museums when they just wanted to spend a day at the beach or vice versa. Without your kids, you can go to places that are not 'children-family'.

This is a great time to cross off some things from your bucket list.

Keep a 10-Second Intro

It is most likely that people would ask you about your country and the extent of your trip. So, when you have covered this information, you also need to have a 10-second introduction about yourself. This can cover your hobbies, interests, and other things of interest. It is a gateway for you to open them up and gauge their personality. This will allow you to make new friends more easily and you can connect with them right off the bat. Try to sound as natural as possible, and avoid the rehearsed speech.

Tip: If nothing comes to mind, be sure to talk good things at length about the host country and this will set them at ease to talk freely about the ins and outs of their country. Talk to them like you have known them for years and they can let you in on a lot of secrets.

Unlearn Stranger Danger

This is something that is on high alert during your solo trips. It has been ingrained into us since childhood. As a solo traveler, chances are that you will be defensive and closed with most of the strangers you meet. It is interesting to note that most of the people you meet during your travels are nice people.

So, keep an open mind and consider strangers as people you haven't met. The word 'stranger' has negative connotations and creating arbitrary walls around yourself is playing safe, but it also closes long-term opportunities right off the bat. Many people would offer you tips and advice only when you have created a level of comfort with them.

People love, hurt, and cry just the same. People have emotions. Find common ground with them and strike a conversation with them and check out the magic that unfolds right in front of you.

Alcohol within Limits

As a solo traveler, you need to understand the essentials of safe traveling. Alcohol is one of them. Understand your tolerance about drinking. This does not just for the ladies, but getting drunk on a solo trip is nothing short of hazardous. As you attempt to regain sobriety, you will lose precious hours of tourism and it also does not go well with your traveling buddies — they could be holed up alongside you.

So, know your limits and work out a level that is not tipsy enough and borders 'wasted level'. Make sure you have a good time whilst traveling and be responsible at the same time. This comes first.

For many reading this, this may sound like sorcery, right? It is hard at first blush, but it is very much possible!

Learn to Smile

A big, confident, and winning smile is a must to keep spirits high and transmit some of that infectious energy onto others. This is a good tip to create some coziness with fellow travelers and people in the country. They will complement the smile and then, they will be quite comfortable talking, laughing, and sharing secrets. This quite a viable tip to keep in mind and works like a charm as well. Smiles are inviting, friendly, and universal. They are understood in all languages and helps break the ice between strangers.

Get Deliberately Lost

At times, it is easy to be inundated by the information related to travel. A million thoughts are running through your mind and people stress about it in varied capacities. This may not sit well with many, but wandering during day/night can give you an enchanting experience and stories.

Some people do deliberately take these strolls without maps or anything. They discover things that weren't on guides, but often a beautiful park or pub comes along. So, the more you travel, the more confidence you have of taking up these excursions.

Just beware of mugging!

Avoid Loneliness on These Solo Trips

Keep an open mind and talk to fellow travelers. Be that as it may, solo travelers can find both solo and group travelers. So, if you are lonely, you can find some much-needed company along the way. Don't be nervous — understand that you might not see these people ever again. That goes for you as well. So, don't be shy and talk to people. Some may be responsive and others may not.

They can be great friends for life. You can add them on social media networks and talk to them for years to come. Who knows, you might actually meet interesting people along the way!

There are some options for meeting new people. Try MeetUp.com which shows people based on similar interests and some of them might be headed your way! Other than that, you can also make friends at hostels. Hostels have a vibrant social atmosphere, and it is a place where people can be at ease and cozy up with others.

Hello has Infinite Power

An interesting quote that I found was, 'I greet the janitor the same as my boss'. This is such great advice and goes for traveling, too. At the inside, we are all more or less similar, human. By being human and treating people with kindness, you add good karma to your collection and keep yourself open to new possibilities and perspectives.

Some people do believe that good things return in different shapes and forms. The energy they create in the system comes back to them and benefits them.

Dining Solo

You would be surprised to know that dining solo is common in Europe, and so is the case with the US. Don't think for a moment that you would be the odd one out in a restaurant. You may find many like yourself. It is quite common to ask strangers for lunch and dinner. You could have a smörgåsbord in Scandinavia, or rijsttafel dinner in Amsterdam, a paella feast in Madrid, or a spaghetti feed in some Italian city. People with Rick Steves' guidebooks are often an extended family, meeting up as their paths collide during travel.

If you are in a socializing mood, ask for single travelers/people to share the table with you. In a hostel, this concern is taken care of with ease.

If you like to be a loner, then you have a lot to do just on your phone alone. Games, surfing, social media apps — the sky is literally the limit. Cafes are quite peaceful and you can spend lazy afternoons in there.

Evenings

European cities are magical at night — they are safe and welcoming. You will not feel alone when you pass by busy roads, crowded cafes, and other popular landmarks. It is quite an enthralling experience on its own. Evening entertainment has tons of options, from movies, dance performances to concerts. Some cities also offer night tours like London or Paris.

If available, book a room with a balcony that overlooks the central city. It is a great sight and a terrific memory to cherish years afterward.

Don't forget to take advice from people, chances are some may have ideas that are right up your alley.

Public Transportation

Exercise the same caution as you do in your homeland for buses and subways. Think about daytime travel for arrival and departure, especially for long-distance routes. Visit the bus station, train stops and airport terminals to make a mental map of their layouts. This will help you later on. Reconfirm the time of departure and if the bus/train station seems to be shady, look for a café in the area or wait in the hotel's lounge.

Now, let's move on to:

Must-have Apps for Solo Travelers

As a solo traveler, your handheld phone is your best companion, caretaker, travel planner, and lifeline. You need to be ready and have the right apps on your phone to keep yourself safe and informed.

This section has listed much-needed apps for solo travelers from different categories.

Download them and consider them your companions for the incoming trip.

Note that a number of these solo travel apps require the creation of an account, profile setup, location tracking to be turned on, and other fussing around, too. Keep some time aside to take care of this before you leave home.

Much-needed Safety Apps for Solo Travelers

First and foremost, staying safe is the most important thing for any solo traveler.

TripWhistle (iOS) helps find the 911 equivalent in other countries. It will call in the local emergency line and share your location with them (let's hope it never comes to that).

The RedZone Map app is really handy. It provides you the safest route in any part of the world. For this, it takes into account the crime statistics and social data. The app also keeps track of incidents in real-time and offers you alternatives to keep you safe. It draws its information from a small subset of user base at the moment. Give it a trial run in your city and check out its accuracy.

My Safetipin (iOS/Android) is an Indian app and only available in five countries as of now. It assesses the area based on nine parameters and generates a safety score. The parameters include density, population density, lighting, among others. It also features a night mode that highlights unsafe areas at night. It will notify the law enforcement authorities if you are in trouble.

Translation Apps

Language barriers are always looming when you are headed to a foreign destination — having no companions to fill in the gaps can be problematic. Google Translate (iOS | Android) is pretty popular among solo travelers, while Microsoft Translator (iOS | Android) has been gaining traction lately, too. This way, you know the businesses that serve splendid gourmet coffee, mouthwatering steaks, or just light munchies.

'Eat with a Local' Apps

A mediocre meal and loneliness isn't exactly anyone's idea of a memorable trip. Thankfully, the app 'eat with a local' is a godsend in this regard. Another great option is VizEat — it has a broader range of options apart from just capital cities. So, you have more to work with every time you head off to a different location.

Eatwith is an app that connects with locals in the area from over 130 countries. Immerse in your favorite cuisine while chatting with a local about the delicacies of his country. The app has events on cooking classes, food tours, dinner parties, and other culinary events. Wine and dine with the local hosts. You can even filter the food options — ranging from vegan, kosher, and vegetarian meals.

Social Networking Apps

Meeting new people and chatting with them isn't everyone's cup of tea, but it's their loss. You should always talk to travelers during your trips, it is so refreshing and engaging. You can find countless apps to find like-minded fellow travelers. One of the most renowned and best apps for solo travelers is Meetup (iOS | Android), operating in many countries right now. On a random search of the area, you can find groups meeting together for bike rides, hikes, empty nesters, coding, single gamers, and so much more. It was a revelation, to be honest.

Tinder (iOS | Android) is another option. To be honest, it is a dating app, but people also use it to find companionship during their travels, especially those who are alone. Tinder has launched a feature that connects people for activities. Check it out!

If you need just travel-related apps, go for SoloTraveller (iOS | Android), Yonder (iOS | Android), Backpackr (iOS | Android), and Travello (iOS | Android).

Also, SoloTraveller is a widely and trusted used app to make friends during your trips. You can connect with other solo backpackers in the city. Save money by pairing up with people — share travel expenses, taxies, and even food expenses. Select your favorite travel mate by filtering people based on age, gender, and common interests.

The app is available on both Android and iOS platforms.

Backpackr is kind of like Tinder, but for the lonesome travelers. The app will list people with similar interests headed to your vacation spot. If it works for you, you may message the individual and ask him to meet up. It is pretty easy to work with and earns some brownie points for deals on restaurants, bars, pub crawls, hostels, and local tours. It is available on both Android and iOS platforms.

The Chirpey app is just for the ladies out there. Yes, women do go on solo trips and it's quite common

So, Chirpey is an online community for the female lot. The members can link up with others and head on a trip together. If you have lost your wallet, then drop a message and some woman in the area will be notified about your problem.

The app is available on both Android and iOS platforms.

Tour and Activity Apps

Feeling alone in a foreign land? You can always take a group tour and strike a conversation with fellow travelers. One solid app to find tour-related activities is Peek (iOS or Peek.com) — it was also recommended by Melinda Gates recently. You can find a ton of stuff to do with this app. When the options are too many to choose from, select the 'handpicked activities just for you' feature. This feature shortlists the list of options from 100 to 33 (depending on the location). The options are auto-generated based on the profile that you create at the time of sign-in. So, be very specific with the app to get the best results.

Next on the list is The Outbound app (iOS or TheOutbound.com). This app is spectacular. It generates superb results not only for the major cities, but also for remote islands, suburban areas, and more. You would be surprised to know that you can find new-to-me places even in your hometown. How cool is that?

Lodging Apps

Some lonesome or snobby solo travelers might prefer to hole up in their room or book a room on the high floor. Other solo travelers prefer lodging options that give them access to the locals in the area. They can meet new people this way. Couchsurfing (iOS | Android) and Airbnb (iOS | Android) is a great way to meet new people by living in their accommodation. You might get a few freebies from some kind hosts.

Hostelword (iOS | Android) is for those who wish to stay in a hostel during their travels. It is a safe option.

Map Apps

This is an important tip for the solo travelers. You should know where you are headed — safety and efficiency play a huge role when you are abroad. You cannot always rely on a steady internet connection and/or mobile data to reach your destination without any hiccups. You can find a truckload of mapping apps. Google Maps (iOS | Android) should be your first choice. Lesser renowned apps are CityMaps2Go (iOS | Android), and MAPS.ME (iOS | Android). Save your map ahead of time, download the directions, and don't worry that much about the data charges.

Photo Apps

The Lightroom app is available on both iOS and Android platforms. The renowned photo editor tool is 'the world's best editing tool' and it is completely free. Of course, some features are paid, but you still have a hell of an editing app for free. Your daily snaps will look stunning.

***

Pro-tip: Keep in mind that all of these apps require the usual procedure of account creation, location tracking, and other messing around. Be sure to leave aside one day for this activity — it requires your undivided attention.

Also, I would suggest keeping a backup phone in case you are mugged in a foreign country. The replacement phone should have all the information so that you are still on track and can contact people back at home. You can buy a ton of mid-end and low-end Android devices/iPhones. Remember — you have spent weeks planning your trip and nothing would be as traumatizing as losing your only phone with everything in it. Play it smartly and transfer the travel-related information in the backup phone. It'll only take a few moments to get this done.

Chapter 9: Bon Voyage — Score Great Bargains on Overseas Getaways

Does the term 'budget holiday' ring any bells? Everyone likes to save thousands of dollars on holidays, and that is completely fine. All that you need to do is find travel itineraries that are worth your while and make the most out of your disposable income. Thankfully, we have done the legwork in that department, too. So, be it just a group of friends or an extended family making this trip, it will feel like a breeze.

Travel your heart out and cherish these memories for years to come when circumstances become more difficult to travel. A few thousand dollars are more than enough for a short, weeklong trip.

You can even squeeze in countries from Southeast Asia if you wish for a month-long stay.

Of course, individual research never hurts and the listed destinations are fan favorites. So, without further ado, let's get to it.

The cities that are shortlisted are categorized according to the continent in which they are located. As you may notice, different cities are renowned for different reasons.

The Asian Belt

New Delhi, India

From the historic bazaars of the colonial times to the modern skyscrapers and subway systems of New Delhi, the city is full of surprises. It is a springboard to embark on a full-on Indian tour. The tourists arrive in New Delhi since the city is a Launchpad for the Golden Triangle, comprising of 3 highly-visited cities — Jaipur, Agra, and the capital city itself. The Taj Mahal and Mehrangarh Fort are the two landmarks over here.

Although organized tours work, you are better off with a rental car and a guide. The cost of accommodation is remarkably low — it is almost pocket change for westerners.

Nepal

A little speck on the world map, situated between India and China, Nepal is a world of its own. It is surprisingly one of the cheapest holiday destinations even today. With its snow-capped Himalayas, hilltop villages, dense jungle plains, rugged mountains, and 10 sites on the World Heritage list, it is a complete package for any tourist.

Amazingly, Nepal is all set up to entertain solo travelers and groups with organized hiking, Annapurna Circuit, and beds along with tea in houses.

For the fans of wildlife, visit Chitwan National Park and see elephants and tigers up, close, and personal. The cost of accommodation is very reasonable.

The capital city Kathmandu is a busy metropolis and a complete shock after the tranquil countryside. Visit the pagodas, pavilions, and savor the delicious food. You can find hotels in your budget easily. From local lodgings to 3-star hotels, you have plenty of options to mull them over.

Turkey

It is a country, where the west meets the east. A seat of civilization and empires, your first stop should be Istanbul. Try their street food, Balik Ekmek, which is a fish sandwich that costs a few dollars.

The world-famous Hagia Sophia is a must-visit landmark. Tourists may know it as 'Blue Mosque', though it was a church during the Byzantine era. The Ottoman Empire converted the structure into a mosque. You can visit the 1,500-year-old mosque with a five-day Museum Pass, which has discounts on major attractions.

Apart from the historic surprises in store, the tourists have golden beaches on the Mediterranean and Aegean coasts. The locals are very friendly and you will fit in right away.

The price of accommodation is mid-range, so pick your poison carefully.

Jeju Island, South Korea

The largest island in Korea is open for travelers, with flight prices and hotel prices remarkably lower than the last year.

Land on the island and head over to the Hyeopjae Beach for a getaway. The mighty Pacific Ocean lies in front of you. The Jungmun Beach is another spot which offers watersports, the likes of which includes rafting, water skiing, parasailing, scuba diving, and yacht tour. These are pretty exciting activities under the sun. Near the shore are some cliffs which house habitat of rare species.

Thanks to its picturesque scenery, the beach has featured in mainstream movies and TV shows. No surprises there!

There is Seongsan Ilchulbong, an extinct tuff volcano, which is 597-foot high. The fee for hiking is very nominal for adults and children, something that won't thin out your wallet.

The Jeju Folk Village is a cultural tour while the Manjanggul Lava Tube is a 5-mile cavern with stalactites and volcanic shelves.

The Southeast Asian Belt

Laos

Laos is an underrated traveler's paradise, and more inexpensive when compared to Myanmar and Thailand. For a light charge, you can stay at the top hotels in the country and have mouthwatering food at your disposal.

The country offers terrific sights for the sore eyes. Buddhist architecture is a huge calling card in the country. As English is surprisingly spoken by a mass majority of the people, finding your way through the country isn't that difficult.

Vietnam

It has the best food in Southeast Asia while the country is staggeringly beautiful. Vietnam remains a highly preferred budget travel destination. For a surprisingly small cost, you have tantalizing food, a guest accommodation, transport and a couple of rounds of beers to go along with it.

Don't forget to try Bia Hoi, a Vietnamese brew and very popular one at that.

Just step up the range a bit and enjoy your stay at Hanoi Serenity Hotel, which is a bang for your buck. Salty broth and fresh rice noodles are a dime a dozen over here.

Hanoi also has some French cruise to offer. Savor the croissants and patisseries along with pho noodle soup shacks.

Visit the Hoan Kiem Lake where the locals practice tai chi at dawn. The rural life of Vietnam is nothing short of splendid either.

Bali

Any urban individual may have come across the name Bali at some time in their lives. It is pretty popular among Aussie tourists due to its geographic proximity to Australia. The island is a solid pick for holidaying at any time of the year. Just to give you an idea, 80% of the economy is based on tourism and a bulk of that tourism is from Australia alone. Bali forms a portion of the Coral Triangle, so it is home to beautiful coral and marine species, too, and much more diverse than the Caribbean Sea.

So, for the Aussies, a trip to Bali is their best bet for a summer excursion. The price of accommodation isn't that steep either.

Thailand

For the travelers on the international circuit, Thailand tops the list in Southeast Asian destinations. Bangkok ranks high on the bucket list of most travelers. A mix of 'old and the new', it is a complete traveler's package, offering historic landmarks and modern architecture. The city has something for everyone, from tourist traps to Buddhist sites, extravagant shopping, public gardens, museums, palaces, and of course the beaches. Though it has acquired some notoriety for being dangerous for the tourists, the footfall of tourists seems to be unaffected by it.

Bangkok is high on the list of Asian travelers, given the cheap tickets and geographic proximity. The cost of accommodation is a breeze. There is a reason tourism contributes a major figure in the Thai economy.

Must-have Apps for Southeast Asia

Grab

It is the Asian equivalent of Uber and Careem. Time is of the essence and if you are no expert in bargaining with the local cab drivers, then save your breath. Just book a Grab and reach your destination stress-free.

Again, the ride-sharing app is primarily for the Southeast Asian audience. You have the option to book a GrabCar, GrabBike, GrabTaxi, GrabFamily, JustGrab, GrabShare, GrabHitch, and GrabExpress. GrabShuttle books your seat on a bus while GrabExpress delivers packages to different locations.

Grab is currently operating in Malaysia, Singapore, Vietnam, Indonesia, Myanmar, Thailand, and Cambodia.

GlobeConvert

Southeast Asia comprises of countries with different currencies. You shouldn't waste any more time than needed on keeping track of your spending. This is where GlobeConvert can help you work out your spending easily. Just type in the new figure and erase the previous one. Simple! Keep it connected to the internet so that it works with the latest exchange rates.

Maps.Me

For the travelers, Maps.Me is the most important application. GMaps doesn't even come close to this one. You can download the map of an entire region on the phone, and use it offline as you like. This saves you hefty roaming bills during your trip. The maps are open sources — the users update it as they like. From evening entertainment to great restaurants, you will find something that will strike a chord with you. Keep the points of interest to explore them at a convenient time. The map is designed specifically for Southeast Asian markets.

Eatigo

If there was a ranking system for the food apps, Eatigo would rise to the top. As a restaurant reservation app, it is the best of the lot. The best feature it has is the stellar discounts of up to 50% — a sweet deal for any frugal traveler.

After the download, you are shown categories. Select from the top 50, types of food, new restaurants among other options. So, select the restaurant and make a booking through the app. The discount will be applied when you receive the bill.

The app is available in India, Hong Kong, Malaysia, Singapore, Philippines, and Thailand.

Hostelworld

The hostels are cheaper than hotels so we suggest booking hostels if you are a frugal traveler. They keep your expenses down.

Hostelworld has built a name for itself in the hostel industry. The app is neat, easy to use, and gives you an array of options right away. The cancelation option is easy because plans do change during trip planning.

The European Belt

Spain

While the rest of Europe is a pricey proposition, Spain takes the market for style and budget travel. The Spanish architecture, food, and culture do not disappoint and the hospitality of Spanish people never goes unappreciated either. So, you are bound to see Europeans over here and Americans as it is a budget tour for most.

The flight pricing is moderate, though it could be different for people from other countries depending on your currency exchange rate.

The cost of accommodation is remarkably inexpensive, even in cities like Barcelona and Madrid. Rooms that are low cost are pretty great during the offseason.

Just avoid the seasons of July and August when footfall is at its peak.

Ireland

Europe is laden with tourist destinations and one for the savvy customers is Ireland. The capital city of Dublin is quite expensive for any frugal traveler's liking, the countryside will certainly compensate for it. You can explore the Irish museums for free — they are all free for that matter and spend minimal time in Dublin.

The lush countryside is instant relief for the sore eyes. You can drive for 120 miles and indulge in the magnificent scenery of the Ring of Kerry. Then don't forget the Killarney National Park, which is a paradise for any walker out there. For just a little over one hundred dollars a night, spend a day or two in the Great Killarney Hotel. They tend to spoil their customers, so be warned!

Then, head towards the smaller B&Bs, they have amazing deals on food and accommodation. On the other hand, restaurants and pubs offer great food and a superior all-round experience. It is worth the visit.

Prague, Czech Republic

Prague has everything for a tourist — a hub of culture and history and a price tag that seems doable for any frugal travelers. The mid-10th

century fort is also here, and Old Town which is a century-old marketplace. Even the Charles Bridge that belongs to the heyday of the Roman Empire is in this city.

The museums in Prague give a crash course in the cultural history of the city. The fourth and fifth symphony of Beethoven is also in the Lobkowicz Palace. The Jewish Museum has 100,000 books and 40,000 exhibits, making it the biggest resource of Jewish culture throughout the ages.

There is something for the beer lovers here, too. The city has terrific brews produced by the Czechs. These Czechs have been at it since the Middle Ages.

Must-have Apps for Europe

Find priceless culinary hotspots, to the perfect cobbled street worth posting on Instagram, and spots that routine crowd usually misses. Stand out from the crowd and take the most memorable European trip ever with these handy apps.

So, if you plan to hit Europe this year, these (free) apps will be a godsend during your journey.

Onefinestay

It is a comprehensive lodging app that provides you much-needed and immediate details. Not only it curates homes and apartments in Rome, Paris, and London, but it also suggests nearest ATMs, hospitals, public attractions, and local restaurants. Download it before departing and fill in the necessary details.

Pretty Streets

If you wish to take a memorable stroll down one of those European streets then this app is for you. It has detailed itineraries of Paris, London, and Dublin's most mesmerizing avenues, boulevards, and streets. The maps are easy to understand and follow. You can also adjust the length of your length — after all, you are on a clock, too.

Fly Europe

This app brings to you the cheapest airfares to and from Europe. It compares the ticket pricing from major and less renowned carriers. Apart from that, it also searches fares from several sites, the likes of which include eDreams, Expedia, and Vayama.

GoEuro

Another comprehensive travel app that allows you to look and book trains, flights, and buses in over 12 European countries. Choose from

3,000 airports and 80,000 bus and railway stations. Imagine the options you have in life!

Spotted by Locals

Nothing is more trustworthy than word of mouth. This app costs $3.99, but it's worth more than its price. Local photographers and writers regularly update their favorite suggestions. The app has vital information on most frequented European cities. So, if you are headed to one of the major cities of Europe, be sure to get this app.

TheFork

The app lists 30,000 restaurants from 10 European countries. Every listing has photos, user reviews, and menu items. The app has a loyalty program and in-app discounts. It's a sweet deal, trust me!

Michelin Travel

You would be surprised to know that the Michelin Guide is a bible of hospitality in Europe. Once you download the (free) app, a world of hotels, best restaurants, and public attractions open up to you. Travelers can book their favorite hotels or restaurants right from the app. It's so convenient.

Citymapper

It's a wonderful navigation tool and displays public-transit information in real-time. Check out the costing and live departure time of trains and buses. You can even find the best seat available on the train. How about that?

You can even share your live location to let the friends know the route you are taking right now.

Monument Tracker

This app covers 60 cities, so you have a comprehensive list of historic gems and renowned monuments in Europe. The app has set itineraries, so you don't need to stick to them all the time. Just activate your GPS and it will alert you to sights in your area.

TripLingo

Many language apps can keep you abreast of the key phrases used in every country. But TripLingo gives you inside information on the informal and slang vocabulary used by the locals. One of the notable features is the instant voice translation feature. Mingle with the locals, throw some slang into the conversation and check how fast they drop their guard.

The Central American Belt

Cook Islands

Located in Central America, the Cook Islands are comparable to Tahiti and Fiji in terms of value addition. This small group of islands is thronged by New Zealanders and Australians — it is their ideal holiday spot.

The lovely islands are renowned for white-sand beaches, gin-colored water, amazing seafood, and locals who are never tired of the travelers. Solo travelers, honeymooners, and families are also well-accommodated for that matter.

Be sure to visit these islands, they have fewer footfalls compared to Tahiti and Fiji, but they are sure to give a bang for your buck.

Nicaragua

In recent years, Nicaragua has become a popular destination for backpackers — it is every frugal traveler's paradise. On arrival, you have a ton of things to do. You can take a tour of the colonial cities, visit any 19 volcanoes in the country, head over to the gorgeous beaches in the country, and take a boat ride in San Juan River. The ticket prices are remarkably low and you can take a group of friends along for a memorable trip.

Amazingly, the cost of accommodation in Nicaragua is so low, it is virtually free. For any hotel/lodging, the price is astonishingly inexpensive while Airbnb costs is either double or, in some cases, more than double.

The ideal time to go is in the bracket of May to October when the rainy season is in full swing. An overclouded weather and picturesque locations would be simply a paradise for many. The country is no less than a bargain at other times of the year as well.

Antigua

Generally less renowned than other hotspots in South America, Guatemala has incredible weather all-round the year. It is a blissful escape for those balmy, summer days and keeps you cool as you tour the country. The historic landmarks are one of a kind here. Be sure to check out the Mayan ruins and active volcanoes. Guatemala has everything for people of all ages.

The luxury hotels are a bit out of the range, though mid-range hotels charge is—much more reasonable for a night. You can relish the wonderful view of forests and volcanoes.

Honduras

If you wish to tour the Maldives again, but lack the funds for it, Honduras is still there as a backup option. It has a lineup of white-sand beaches and it is perfect for the honeymooners as well. So, for less than $50 a day, you have extravagant hotel rooms, fine dining at your disposal. The Eco Hotel Shanghai La is a 3-star with lavish pools, gardens, and also a bar to relax after the daylong excursion.

It is also a fantastic option for scuba diving and the training courses are offered at dirt-cheap rates. The northern coast of Honduras has pristine beaches and is ideal for snorkeling, too.

The colonial city of Comayagua is a splendid sight for the sore eyes. Soak in the beautiful Spanish houses and town-center plazas. Grab a bite at one of the cafes in the city and enjoy a good meal without much out of pocket expense.

North American Belt

Calgary, Canada

A beautiful city in Canada, its landscapes never ceases to mesmerize incoming tourists. While for some, it is just a stopover en route to Banff, it is a perfect weekend getaway.

The Hawthorn Dining Room & Bar and Fairmont Palliser are quite renowned while the New Central Library is practically free for entry. Take in the architecture of the library, followed by a stroll over the Peace Bridge. Rafts are there for rental from Lazy Day Raft Rentals.

The bars in Calgary are a major draw for the tourists as each cocktail bar brings its flavor and adds more charm to the city.

The African Belt

South Africa

The country is a fantastic base destination if you wish to tour Africa someday. Though it is by no means the cheapest of the lot, it sure has appreciable value addition for any tourist. With its wildlife, vibrant cities, unspoiled beaches, and so much more, the fun never stops. Cape Town has been recently ranked numerous times as the best destination for travel in Africa in the World Tourism Awards of 2019.

United Airlines has added Cape Town to its flight list, so now it is a direct flight from Newark to Cape Town. This has brought in competition as other airliners jump the bandwagon.

For American travelers, Cape Town is quite affordable, and they have a lot more for your top dollar. It is known for renowned wines, restaurants, and souvenirs to bring home.

Morocco

At the crossroads of Europe and the Middle East, Morocco never ceases to amaze westerners. The land has stunning scenery, fascinating culture, and throwaway shopping prices. The Marrakech city is your base destination, from where you can explore other parts of the country. Flights to African countries aren't overly expensive, but it is a reasonable price for the exchange of experience.

The price of accommodation is a notch high compared to other cities on the list. However, you'll still be pleasantly pleased that you won't have to shell out very much money for a night stay. The two slots for Morocco are from March-April and September-December.

Africa: Live

This app is as amazing as they come. It has won the best travel app within the African domain. You can share real-time wildlife sightings on live maps and update their location. You can follow the trail of other safari-goers who posted their wildlife sighting and follow their lead. The wonderful app is available on both [iOS](iOS) and Android platforms.

ParkSpotter Africa

If national parks are on your list, then you definitely need to have this app on your mobile, pronto.

It will help you in Addo National Park, Kruger National Park, Kgalagadi Transfrontier Park, Etosha National Park, and Table Mountain National Park. It'll provide you all the necessary information about the parks, such as:

- Hiking routes
- Points of interests
- Waterholes
- Gate opening times
- Park contact details
- Flora and fauna information

XE Currency Converter

It is an amazing currency converter app that you can use on-the-go. Yes, you have a lot on your plate during vacations. This app is handy because you may need to convert the currency repeatedly to gauge the price of a product/service. So, it is better to know about the price you are going to pay for something rather than regret it later. This app is free of cost and updates its exchange rates throughout the day. It has nearly all currencies.

Duolingo

For foreigners taking a trip to East Africa, the language barrier will soon become problematic for them to maneuver. So, download the Duolingo app first. The app is well-designed and works great if you are trying to learn a language, need to exchange a few words or give some instructions.

The app is free to use and available on both Android and iOS platforms.

Weather Underground App

Nothing is more upsetting and frustrating than a sudden downpour. The weather apps do have data on the weather forecast based on regions, but you need something better than that. This app has the standard weather details, but it goes a step further than that. It also shares information about wind speed, temperature, weather forecast, cloud cover, humidity, wind direction, and visibility. It will give auto-alerts about impending natural disasters and extreme weather conditions.

Safeture

Heading to East Africa can be a tad bit dangerous. Most of the countries in the East African bloc are safe, but political situations can get unstable at times.

Download Safeture — it is a free-to-use app and gives you a heads up on the conditions in unstable regions. It has reliable sources at its disposal, so you don't need to worry about cross-checking the information.

It is a must-have app on your phone because it has data on safety warnings, natural disasters in the pipeline, and contact information of the local emergency units.

The app is free to use, so don't think twice about downloading it.

GMaps

If you need to know your way on the streets (car or on foot), GMaps are your best bet. You can also avoid the cab drivers who usually rip off the tourist. It's a reality that you need to understand and if it sounds harsh, that's because it is.

Google Translate

Do you need a crash course in Arabic or Hebrew? Google Translate is here for you. You can translate the signs, menus, and restaurant names with convenience.

So, if it's a coffee shop you wish to enter, then it WILL be a coffee shop. You can also use the voice tool to directly translate speech as well.

Gett

It's getting late now and you need to catch a cab? Don't fret! Just download the Gett app and link it with your credit card. So, even if you have no cash on you at the moment, the credit card will come in handy.

Remember to download it before your trip. Make a list of these apps and download them before the trip.

BonJournal

Everything is digital now and you don't exactly need to keep a travel journal. This travel journal app will take care of that. Tag the locations, upload photos or not, it is up to you. Share your adventures with friends and close ones. The journal can be converted to a PDF file, so you can get it printed later.

Chapter 10: Fantastic Voyages – Cruise in Style for Less

Sometimes, the budget can be tight, but you always have options. There are plenty of deals out there that could satisfy your needs if you know how and where to look. Don't just throw away the vacation plans like that. So, if luxury cruises are your thing, some cruise liners certainly fit the bill and have less splashy features than the others.

Compared to the airline industry which is rife with low-cost carriers, cruise lines that are considered low-budget are far and few. Though, some of the older ships like the Norwegian Cruise Line, Royal Caribbean, and Carnival could be pigeonholed into this category.

So, to ease the journey, this section has categorized the cruise lines into 3 categories. This way, travelers can pick their preferences, season, and price points that seem suitable to them. Some cruise lines have lower rates depending on the season and the itinerary they choose. Using savvy strategies, you can even sneak your way into upscale cruise lines and mainstream ships.

So, to make sure that you are getting those insider secrets that avid cruisers know, let's get to the next section.

Budget Cruise Lines

The cruise lines fall into broad price points, but not one qualifies as a budget cruise line. So, it is prudent to look for sales on older ships that work with these mainstream cruise lines.

Bahamas Paradise Cruise Lines

This offers a lavish two-night, low-cost cruise starting from the Palm Beach in Florida to the Bahamas. The two ships are named Grand Classica and Grand Celebration. This cruise line targets first-timers looking to test the waters with a cruise line. The fares can be surprisingly inexpensive for a person (before taxes and additional charges) while providing you a nice deal that goes light on your wallet.

These ships are not exactly mega-ships with a load of 1,500 to 1,700 passengers. Once on-board, the cruise line features many restaurants for travelers to indulge in. These range from the poolside grill, steak and seafood venue, the main restaurant, and many bars to relax after a meal.

Apart from these, spa, gym, theatre, casino, and lounges are also available as are hot tubs and pools.

Age-appropriate waterslides and kids' clubs are also available.

Older Ships in Mainstream Cruise Lines

Cruises on relatively older ships have lower charges. This is for two reasons majorly — these ships lack the hype and facilities marketed in the newer models, and these are deployed on routes that are less popular amongst the travelers.

That does not mean that you will have a dull day on the cruise line. No, sir! For a first-timer, you will hardly miss anything — it will feel like a comprehensive tour, complete with facilities of all sorts. Also, don't think that the companies have abandoned these cruise ships either, these are just older models now.

The award for the most economical cruise line goes to Carnival. You should be able to score a four-night cruise without having to shove a lot of cash out of your pocket. The Carnival Victory, which launched back in 2000 is still in use, but still packs a punch nevertheless.

Carnival Imagination and Inspiration ships which launched back in the 1990s have 4-night Mexico cruises for similar prices. Other ships in the category are also sailing on these routes. Majesty of the Seas (1992) is a great bet for budget travelers. Other than that, the Norwegian Spirit (1998) does an 11-night Mediterranean tour for a very reasonable price.

Vacation To Go

Looking for a cruise liner at remarkably low price? Then this is it! Operating in the industry since 1984, Vacations To Go has been in the business of discount cruises for 4 decades.

Cruise ship placements sell like hotcakes, so if you see any cruise that is worth your while, book it right away. The slots fill up in a matter of hours. That just says a lot about its demand. Go to Advanced Search or Find a Bargain to check out some of the best discounts the industry has to offer. Booking is a breeze with them. Feel free to call at 800-338-4962.

Cruise.com

This cruise corporation offers just about everything. It has the best cruise deals in the lineup and offers discounts on different cruise lines and vacation packages. It covers locations worldwide so you might find something that is worth your while depending on the season at hand.

Cruise.com also helps travelers with last-minute cruise deals. Steep discounts are offered on these travel deals and you would be amazed at the places that you can discover at such remarkably low prices. The cruise company covers South America, Asia, Europe, Alaska, Caribbean, Australia, and also full world cruises. With the Cruise.com, the fun never stops.

Affordable Cruise Options for Solo Travelers and Families

CruiseComplete.com

When the website was launched in 2003, it was promised that it would change the way people would go cruise shopping. It has never looked back since that day. Major news portals have covered the giant and the value it brings to the customers with its offerings and service excellence in unmatchable.

It is not in the business of selling travel, but only connects the customers with the cruise options. All the customers have to do is to submit their detailed requirements and other bits of information. The quotes are sent back to the customers who can book their cruises for a specific date. So, this is an interesting option for one and all.

If you like to explore more cruise alternatives in your quest to score the best bargain here are a few additional sites to choose from:

- Cruiseone.com
- CruiseDirect.com
- CostoTravel.com
- CruiseOnly.com
- CheapCaribbean.com
- Cruisewatch.com
- Cruisedaeals.com

Deciding on a cruise line or which ship to take can be complicated, time-consuming and requires some research. To ensure that you are getting the top value on your cruise deal and for inside intelligence on the best vacation and certain amenity offers from cruise lines you should check out online cruise reviews which provides practical tips and information to help you sort through all the things you will need to consider. Although there are quite a few sites out there with cruise reviews, there are a few that stand out from the crowd. One of the best, *Cruisecritic.com* is a leading cruise site that provides consumer news to help you find the right cruise, and plan your trip with confidence. It features reviews of ocean, river, luxury and expedition vessels and share reviews from people who've recently cruised on those ships. The site also offer itinerary and pricing information, deals and money-saving insights and a forum for people to post questions and share experiences with other cruisers. The site allows you to compare cruise prices from other websites and when it's time to book it can facilitate completing your transaction. Even better, if you don't have the time to frequently keep an eye on whether the fare on a cruise you have interest have dropped, you should check out the site's "Price Alert" tracker tool that will notify you when the prices change on a cruise you're been watching.

Just a word of caution about cruise price comparison. When comparing cruise prices you need to keep alert that you are comparing similar deals as cruise line pricing can be tricky. The true value of a cruise will often vary as many lines offer promotions with various perks. You may be able to land a free dinning, beverage, or Wi-Fi package or perhaps free gratuities or extra onboard credit. You should calculate the value to you based on what's included in the offer verses what it may cost you extra. Just make sure that it is in line with your preference to enjoy a better cruise experience.

In addition to cruise critic there are many other quality review sites out there to help experience cruisers or those new to cruising find information about cruise lines, itineraries, and specific cruise ships. The one's we list below are definitely worth a visit:

- CruiseReviews.com
- Cruisemates.com
- CruiseDiva.com
- CruiseLineFans.com
- AllThingsCruise.com

If you are looking for an easy way to keep up to date on the latest cruise promotions and to book a cruise at the best available price, be sure to add social media sites as a resource. For instance, you may be able to Tweet your way to savings by checking on the site for last-minute cruise bargains. Many of the travel agents and cruise booking sites like cruise.com and cruisedeals.com are tweeting some fabulously deals that you don't want to overlook.

Another way to ease the process of booking a cruise is to have deals sent to your inbox. Major cruise lines like Royal Caribbean, Holland America, Norwegian, and Celebrity allow you to sign up for emails where they will send you their promotions in addition to last minute deals and short sales. If you decide to sign up to their site you might want to set up a separate account for these mailings so it won't clutter up your personal email inbox.

Overnight Cruises

These are cruises that won't break your bank. Though you will not find cruises for one or two nights that much. Still, they are great for a short getaway weekend. For instance, Princess Cruises and Holland America have short tour routes for Seattle and Vancouver. The price is generally below $100 per person.

Other than that, Carnival has short tours that are also low cost. It works for just about anyone willing to test the waters with cruise-liners (pun intended). You do not need to spend much time in the cabin since the trip is that short. Food, entertainment, and amenities onboard (nightclub and pool) are all on the house.

Three to Four Night Cruises

Older ships and shorter routes make for excellent options on night cruises. The ships used for these short tours are not that old and still work quite well. They have decent facilities onboard so you do not have to worry about a thing.

Carnival has a full range of short cruises to Baja Mexico, Bahamas, and the Western Caribbean. These cruises are three to four-night cruises. Cruises for Cuba and the Western Caribbean are also available. So, options are a lot in that region.

Norwegian Sky also has short trips to Cuba and the Bahamas. Alcohol is also part of the deal so you can enjoy more onboard.

Search for prices under $300/ person. Anything slightly above $100 or below is also a good deal. The Cuba cruises are slightly expensive but they are worth it if you can handle the price tag. The party atmosphere is prevalent onboard since short trips attract the younger lot.

Repositioning Cruises

Wait, is that even a thing?

Sure it is! Repositioning cruises are those that have a different embarkation port and a different disembarkation port. These cruises are less common because most ships have the same starting point (from where they began) and the nightly rates are quite low-priced. These are one-way routes taken by the ships when it moves from one area to another. These trips are comparatively pricier than shorter trips because these cruises extend beyond one week.

The trips are mostly taken when the warm-weather cruise season either starts or ends. These trips attract retirees and mature travelers for whom time is not an object. Trips are over ten days long which is why the crowd is different in these cruises.

Take voyages that start from U.S. East Coast, Florida, and the Caribbean to Europe. They usually stop at Azores or Canary Islands on their way. Once you arrive at the West Coast, you can find sailings that go to Alaska, southern California homeports (and in some cases, Australia, Asia, and Hawaii). Panama Canal voyages are also available for tourists between Florida and California.

The length of the itineraries that extend over seven days or more at the sea is a great cost-saver.

It lowers the nightly rates, making this deal ideal for first-timers to test the waters (pun intended) with cruise-liners. The airfare is still remarkably high if you were to fly to these locations.

Next up is Holland America which has attractive deals. If you're looking for a good buy, you can grab a two-week transatlantic trip from Rome to Fort Lauderdale at prices much lower than you might think.

Its ships are not even old, actually.

The Solstice-class ships of Celebrity are also low-priced. The repositioning cruise on Norwegian Gem for ten-nights, covers Canada to New England while Explorer of the Seas by Royal Caribbean goes from Dubai to Barcelona both of which you can snatch some amazing deals.

For those who want something shorter and low-cost, check out the Pacific Coastal cruises during fall and spring seasons. These ships sail to Alaska and return.

Budget Seasons for Cruise Lovers

If you wish to visit a destination and save money while you are it, browse the seasonal discounts. The shoulder seasons (the off-seasons for cruising) are quite pocket-friendly for budget cruise-lovers. The tradeoff for these budget tours is the unlikeable weather. But you will always prefer fewer people onboard and unaffordable airfare over that any other day, right?

Alaska during May and September

You can now cruise Alaska at a price of your choice. Be sure to choose the month of May or September for sailing. The ship leaves for warmer climates.

Since the flowers, aquatic life, and animals are less abundant and the weather is colder, these cruise periods are less popular for other visitors. Tourists prefer the months from June to August for sailing across Alaska. The rates drop for the less popular months remarkably. The plus point of sailing in May is that it rains less at this time of the year. In September, you can watch aurora borealis from your naked eye.

Mexico, Bahamas, and Caribbean during Fall Season

Autumn is the bargain month for budget cruise-lovers — that goes for any region as well. The lowest offerings are that of the Bahamas and the Caribbean. During the shoulder season, you can easily find incredible deals per person for a seven-day cruise. Cruises for three to five days are also quite affordable.

The low prices are mostly due to the Christmas season and Labor Day, but also because of the hurricane season in the Atlantic Ocean (most of the hurricanes occur from August to October). Purchase travel insurance to protect yourself from hurricanes and canceled cruises/delayed sailings because of unstable weather.

Mediterranean in Winter Season

Many ships take off for the Mediterranean during the fall season and return in spring. Now ships prefer to stay in November and return in March. Some cruises even prefer to roam the European waters during winters.

The spring and fall seasons are wonderful for a family cruise across Europe. However, late-fall and early-spring seasons are dicey. Due to this reason, winter cruises are at their lowest at this time. Cruises set for the Mediterranean region and the Canary Islands in winter can be really inexpensive r per person. Kids can be free of cost (if they are 11 years or below 11 years).

Chapter 11: Smart Safety and Healthy Tips for Worry-Free Travel

Stress-free travel, is that even a thing? It is for those who prefer to travel on familiar paths, closer to home. But where is the fun in that? If you are willing to take a leap of faith and go the distance (pun intended), you need to know some smart and healthy tips for safe traveling. Once you have done the legwork, your mind will be at peace — you will have new-found confidence as great adventures await you!

In this chapter, we will cover some smart safety and health-related tips for travelers — be it automobiles, trains, subway, or airplanes — you need to exercise caution. Airports are stressful because airports have increased health and security checks than before. On the other hand, when you are traveling, you will be using public restaurants, restrooms, and silverware.

So, compiled below are the top tips on safety and health-related advice from frequent travelers — be it on the road or the air. Read on!

Purchase Travel Insurance

You have booked the flight, a hotel, and set a budget for miscellaneous expenses. Should you throw travel insurance into the mix, too? Is it that necessary? To determine that, you need to ask yourself these questions first:

The Frequency of Your Travelling

Suppose you are leaving for New York City next week, then there is no need for the insurance. You will be able to make the trip.

If your trip is slated for next year, then get the insurance first thing. The travel insurance will cover you in case of loss/theft, catastrophic loss, or if you have become incapacitated.

Handling Loss of the Money and Thinking of Cancellation

Trip to New York City — you will lose $500 and that is fine.

Trip to Galapagos Islands — you could lose $10,000 but you could go at another time as well.

The Possibility of Injury and Illness during the Trip

For New York City — the American health insurance has got you covered.

For Grand Canyon — the American insurance will cover you but your evacuation costs will not be covered by the plan.

Galapagos — it is highly unlikely that the American insurance will cover you there and evacuation costs are separate.

Considering the risks that come with heading to far-flung areas, it is better to have travel insurance for you and the kids. The pain of a child is unbearable after all.

As a tourist, you should always have property and health insurance during traveling. Unexpected events do happen and they are well beyond your wildest imagination.

Worlds Nomads is a good option as travel insurance for short-term (travel for below 6 months). You can buy it easily online. It offers good value for international and domestic travel and provide 24/7 emergency assistance, emergency medical coverage, trip cancellations, gear and more.

For those who are traveling for longer than 6 months, they need a mix of insurance options to keep them covered. IMG provides great health insurance and TCP Photography Insurance provides computer/photography.

Seek Local Advice

If you wish to find about the safe neighborhoods and those that are sketchy, you need to know a local in the area. A few locals for confirming information is even better. For the most part, locals are friendly and they will warn you about dangerous areas. Again, have a second and third opinion about the places to keep it safe for yourself (and your family).

Taxi drivers are a fifty-fifty thing. Some information sources are terrific while others misguide you just for fun. Personally speaking, hotel front desk workers have good and reliable information. So, be sure to find all the necessary information about moving around the city without any trouble.

Register with the Embassy

The U.S. Department of State has initiated a Smart Traveler Enrollment Program. It informs the local embassy about your arrival at the destination. The local embassy keeps you informed from that point onwards. It's a free service and accessible for the US-based citizens. This way, you have updated information about the destination and take precautions as necessary.

Canada has 'Registration Of Canadians Abroad' which serves the Canadian citizens. If something out of the ordinary happens, the local embassy will contact the Canadians and direct you to take action for your safety.

Never Overshare with Strangers

Standing in a foreign land, beware of people that come off as overly friendly. Chances are they have an ulterior motive for being that way. Secondly, do not publicly post your tour/itinerary information on social media websites. It could be just the thing that someone with ill-intentions is looking for.

Also, once you have arrived at your destination, never share the travel plans and the accommodation details either. Don't even tell the local shop owner about your current accommodation.

If someone does ask, just lie about your current residence. Since you have researched the area, you will know a few places.

Lastly, when someone asks you about the trip being your first, never confess that. You can say confidently that this is your second or third trip now.

Follow the Dress Code

As a traveler, the wrong dress code screams 'tourist', and that point onwards, you are a potential target for thieves, scammers, and even sexual abuse. The less 'touristy' you look, the less attention you will draw from the wrong crowd.

Donning the right clothes also indicates that you are appreciative of the host country's culture. For instance, the Islamic countries have a certain dress code guidelines which are enforced rather strictly. Many countries have a no-tolerance policy for certain dresses (or lack of it, too). It is illegal to walk topless in the streets of Barcelona (both sexes included). But the local officials can still be offended by whatever you are wearing and create needless hostility in the process. Ignoring the customs of a country comes off as both ignorant and arrogant.

In countries with conservative values, it is better to dress conservatively to draw less attention to yourself. As a foreigner, you will stand out from the crowd, but it will be less dangerous this way.

Check out the general guidelines on Wikipedia regarding the clothing laws of countries. Now you have friends, expatriates, and Facebook groups to ask these questions so you are pretty much covered on that front.

Keep the Bags Tethered

Many 'snatch-and-flee' robberies usually happen because the thief has the motive, means, and opportunity. They have ample time to flee the scene before the owner realizes anything. So, anything that slows their escape is off the table for them.

One thing that you can do to keep your bags safe is to ensure that they are tethered. When your luggage is immovable, the thief will sideline it and look for easier options instead.

Carry a First-aid Kit

This is something that you should always have — yet hope that day never comes. You need to keep one pack in your suitcase, it is an incredibly crucial travel-related item, especially if you are heading to nationals parks or rugged areas. Be it domestic or international travel, you will not have to worry about accidental injuries and mishaps because you have got the kit. In an emergency, it feels like a godsend!

For the road trip, you can pack a small-sized travel first aid kit. You will need Band-Aids, alcohol swabs, plasters, antiseptic cream, sling, different tablets, and syrups. The usual stuff includes motion sickness pills, ibuprofen, Imodium, and paracetamol.

Keep a Sanitizer Kit

You never know the sanitary conditions of gas stations, rest areas, or unfamiliar restaurants for that matter. You cannot leave that to chance — create your private sanitary kit with some bar soaps, sanitizing wipes, and bottle of water to wash. This way, you do not need to worry about the hygiene standard of each rest stop you take during the trip.

If you are driving a rental car, sanitize the interior of the vehicle before you sit inside. Focus especially on the touchpoints like the mirrors, door handles, gear shifts, and steering wheel — these are used mostly by the public. Once this five-minute procedure is done, you can now drive across the country safely.

While you are on the road trip, you will definitely spend the night in on-the-road motels. Prefer those with touch-free technology and handheld devices. Hilton Hotels has this technology and others are also following suit now.

If that is difficult, then use the sanitizer kit to wipe all the necessary touchpoints — TV remote, light switches, accommodation doors, bathroom faucets, and other key touchpoints.

Prescription Medications

Keep the prescription medications in their original pharmacy bottles. Also, snap a photo for safekeeping purposes. Apart from that, keep the prescription medicines that you do not take daily. Do carry the OTC medication that you use occasionally because the weather conditions of certain areas can intensify it. Though pharmacies are mostly open in urban cities, you cannot go around looking for one at midnight!

Never Bring Anything Too Pricey

The first rule of packing — never carry precious jewelry and other valuables. You might want to dress up but pickpockets are known for their sleight of hand — it could be a family heirloom or a wedding gift — they do not care! Jewelry marks you as a wealthy individual in many parts of the poverty-stricken world. Imitation jewelry is the best — if stolen, it does not make the heart heavy. The same goes for branded wristwatches — the high-end ones.

Secure the Bags

You can purchase anti-theft bags but they are not really necessary — that PacSafe camera bag and PacSafe CitySafe bag is quite something though. Any handbag or backpack can be made secure with s-biners to safely lock the zippers, tether the wallet with the safety pin/strap, and take the bag crossbody.

Learn Common Travel Scams

No matter which country you land, you will realize that people will use every trick in the book to steal your cash or valuables. Sometimes, it is obvious and sometimes, it is too long before you realize it has happened. Plenty of con artists are working the tourist traps all the year round.

Note: everyone thinks they cannot be scammed until they are.

Some of the popular travel scams are the 'broken taxi meters' in Costa Rica, milk scam in Cuba, and the renowned ring scam in Paris. Each country has a set of scams that are famous in their region.

Remember: forewarned is always forearmed and this one-hour research will keep you fully informed about tricks played by lowlife conmen. You save yourself from losing money by researching a bit.

When Disaster Strikes

It all happens unexpectedly, you may not have time or the internet to contact the local ambulance service nor the police. In these cases, internet facilities are down at times. You could be too panicky to think straight.

Have an emergency plan before the trip starts. Don't be 'that guy who is scrambling for help at the eleventh hour'. Save it in your phone and keep it in a hard copy as well (it could be a sheet of paper or sticky notes). Use your wallet for accessing it hands-on. This way, you will always know who to call and where to go when things spiral out of control.

No Animal Bites

You may notice stray animals roaming the streets. Stay away from them because they can spread disease. Even puppies and kittens can spread the disease for that matter.

If you are bitten by an animal (or it licks you), wash that affected area immediately with soapy water.

Get the affected area checked by a doctor. If possible, a tetanus vaccine booster or rabies treatment is great.

No Sunburns

- Keep a sunscreen to protect yourself against UVA and UVB rays.
- If you apply insect repellent before a sunburn, reverse the order. Apply the sunscreen first and then apply the repellent.

Avoid Road Accidents

Motor vehicle accidents are the leading cause of the majority of American deaths abroad. Some preventive measures for that are given below:

- Hire a driver temporarily to take you around the city. Now Careem, Lyft, and Uber make things ridiculously easy.
- Never book a ride with a seemingly drunk driver
- Avoid overbooked buses and public transportation
- Wear a seat belt and choose cars that have a seat belt
- Make sure that your car has airbags. Many older versions do not have this feature

Taking these tips into account you still may have a few fears and concerns particularly if you're venturing out into places you've never been before. It's quite natural to have these feelings but it's nothing you can't handle. Here are some other suggestions to follow to protect yourself and ensure a happy and secure journey.

Mind your health

If traveling internationally, check to see if your destination requires vaccinations and if your activities warrant additional immunizations before you leave. If you need medical care while away, your embassies and consulates can help. You should also contact your doctor back home for advice, if that's an option. It's also a good idea to review your health insurance to see if it cover care received abroad. You might want to consider benefits from tour companies and organizations like the American Automobile Association (AAA) and the American Association of Retired Persons (AARP) who offer medical referrals and supplemental insurance discounts.

Keep a copy of emergency information

It's always a good idea to have an emergency plan no matter where you go. If trouble strikes you may be too stressed out to think straight or have time to quickly search for the local police, ambulance or friends/colleagues telephone numbers. Also, you may need to call or find directions to your country nearest embassy but during an incident this information may not be easily available to obtain. You should record emergency numbers in advance and saved it to your notes app on your phone. A written copy should also be kept as a backup just in case your cellphone get lost. This includes copying important documents like your driver's license and insurance. This way, you'll always know who to contact and where to seek help if something go wrong or you find yourself in a jam.

Make a copy of your passport

As you prepare for your trip abroad, scan a copy of your passport, email it to yourself and take a picture of your passport and save it on your cellphone. In the event your passport gets stolen it will make it easier for you to receive a replacement. Moreover, if you happen to be out but left your passport in your hotel while traveling and need it you'll have easy access to all your information.

Share your Itinerary

Once you have determined where and when you are traveling, it's always wise to let someone else know too. This doesn't mean that you should rush to post your itinerary on Facebook or tell everybody you know, particularly strangers. You have to be cautious as someone with ill intentions could use this information against you. Perhaps the easiest way is to email your full itinerary to family or close friends and let them know what your general plans are and when you are expected to return. This way should something come up unexpectedly or they don't hear from you a few days from when you are scheduled to return they can try to contact you to ensure that you are safe or they can help notify the proper local security authorities or embassy.

Maintain situational awareness

As you move about your destination observe and stay situationally aware of your surroundings. Become familiar with any local laws and customs before you depart so you won't be caught off guard and generate hostility against you. Also, be aware of how you dress as the wrong clothes scream tourist and could make you stand out as a possible target for scammers or thieves.

Non-verbal language can come to your rescue in precarious situations. Projection of confidence can keep you safe from being the next victim while on vacation.

Keep your head straight, alert, and up. Beware of everything in your surroundings. Pickpockets can sense your alertness via your body and eye movements.

They will look for an easier victim to rob instead.

In some cases, when you are aware of a potential pickpocket, make eye contact to throw them off their game. But you need to be selective in doing so. Making eye contact in other parts of the world invites trouble right off the bat.

While walking in a foreign country, be confident. Do not look scared, worried, or lost. Also, avoid staring contests with sketchy strangers as much as you can.

Look at the State Department Website

Another useful tip is to look at the U.S. Department of State's website. It has good information about the present threats and known difficulties for American tourists in other countries. One problem is that the State Department lists down all the potential things that can go wrong in these countries. You may encounter something new entirely (which is no one's fault).

This you need to have more in-ground information when you are looking to visit a certain destination. Reading the travel warnings will give you an idea of what is happening inside the country right now. Sometimes the information is dated so make sure you have the current information.

Similarly, never draw overall conclusions. Just because some parts of Mexico or Thailand are problematic, does not mean the rest of the country is a no-go area, too.

Bug Bites

Fleas, ticks, mosquitoes, and some flying insects can spread yellow fever, malaria, dengue, Zika virus, Lyme disease, and chikungunya. These diseases have disastrous consequences.

- Purchase insect repellents that are approved by the EPA. Look for these active ingredients — lemon eucalyptus, IR3535, picaridin, DEET, 2-undecanone, and para-menthane-diol (PMD) should be present.

If you notice flying insects in a certain region, wear full sleeve clothes as much as you can.

Never Use the Back pocket

Pickpockets are everywhere, be it anywhere in the world. As a tourist, you should never use back pockets for wallet, cellphone, or car keys. It is almost tantamount to sitting on a mousetrap. Drop this habit for a few months before you head over to the destination.

Keep your valuables in the front pocket instead. It is below your line of sight and very difficult to steal unless you are sleeping. Use a money belt for destinations where pickpockets are a dime a dozen. Many people hate it but it does the job nevertheless.

Use ATMs Smartly

Now that you are in a foreign country, you will have to use the ATM a bit wisely. Some tips will help in this case. While typing the PIN code of the card, cover the keypad with your hand. This makes it impossible for onlookers to guess what you just entered. It also blocks hidden cameras to record your PIN code as well.

Examine the ATMs before using it. Look at it closely and see any signs of tampering. If you can spot some tampering with the ATM, leave it immediately.

It is better to use ATMs in a supermarket or a shopping mall. People are walking frequently and you have less fear of getting mugged.

Sometimes, the ATM takes your card. In that case, run your finger on the slot to see something extending outwards. The famous 'Lebanese Loop' is a common trick to capture debit cards. It does not let the ATM accept the card, capturing it before it can make its way into the machine. After you walk away in frustration, a thief yanks it out and runs off with it.

If you see a lonesome guy walking around the ATM — having no business — you should leave that ATM and look for an alternate one. If someone wants to 'help' you, do not let them get closer to you! They could have a gun hidden and instruct you to pull out any amount of money they need.

Food and Water Intake

Food poisoning is very, very rare when you are an experienced traveler. From an experienced traveler, here are some tips that will save your hospital rounds in a foreign country.

Try new foods while on vacation, there is nothing like it. New foods are almost always the highlight for people during their vacations. These tips will keep you safe anywhere in the world:

- Prefer places that has a long line of people standing
- Look at how the food is prepared
- Fully cooked food is the best
- Only eat peel-able fruit
- Keep translation cards to show your allergies

Purchase bottled water when you are heading off to remote and rugged areas. In city limits, water is mostly safe to drink, but beyond the city, you never know.

While bottled water is great, you also help with plastic pollution everywhere you go. You can keep one water bottle and reuse it for as long as it's suitable to use.

Chapter 12: Essential Apps to Make Every Journey Easier, Faster, and Hassle-Free

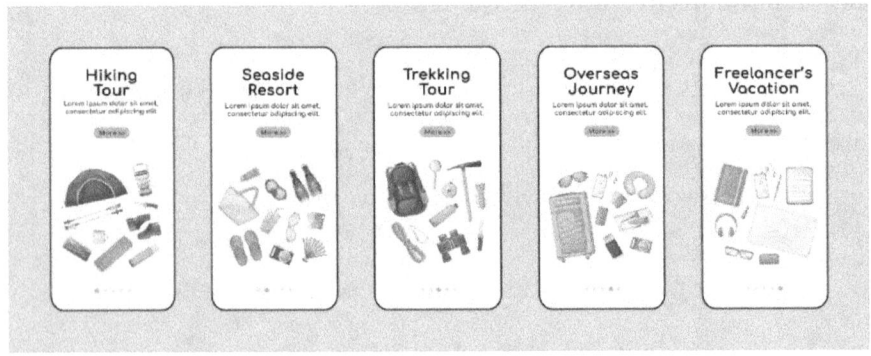

Apps for Headache-Free Trip Planning

As you can see, for many of us, planning a trip and keeping up with all of the details can be stressful if not complicated with the juggling of flight and transportation reservations along with hotel bookings. Luckily there are apps to make trip planning painless. These apps have features that track your flight to suggesting local sights. To save you hassles and time simply forward your travel, hotel, car, or other reservations confirmations and the app instantly creates a single itinerary for you. You will be able to sync your plans to your calendar and easily share them with anyone you choose. No more frantically searching through your inbox when it's time to begin your journey.

Here is some must-have apps that will make staying organize a breeze and let you navigate your way through places like a pro.

Rome2rio — Download the app or visit their website and enter your origin and destination points (city, town, landmark or even an address anywhere in the world) into the search box to help you get directions on the best way to go from A to B, one destination to another. The site will compare and calculate routes by plane, train, bus, car, ferry, bike share, driving and walking directions, in one search, and estimate the price range for each mode of transportation.

TripIt — Helps you manage and keep your travel plans on track as your itinerary falls into place. Just forward your confirmation emails and it will be added to your master itinerary.

Sygic travel — Permits you to create a daily itinerary or a ready to go tour. It makes it easier to discover interesting and popular places. Also, the app provides insightful guides on many popular destinations.

Roadtrippers — Allows you to plan your journey, find the best stops along your route, and lead your way with turn-by-turn navigation. As you plot your itinerary suggestion come up for you to consider or explore.

TripCase — It organizes your trip details and travel plans into a simplified itinerary. It can access eTickets, e-invoices, and itineraries which allows travelers to be more independent while en route.

RedZone Map — If you are traveling solo, safety should be your first and foremost priority. The RedZone Map app lists areas with high crime rates, so you can avoid them conveniently. The app integrates data from government agencies to show the intensity of crime in different areas. It marks the crimes with different colors. Alerts are placed on geo-tagged shootings, thefts, assaults, and other crimes. So, download the app to help you find the safest travel route in a foreign.

Country.Hopper — Traveling solo, you do make last-moment plans. The Hopper app helps you with inexpensive last-minute flights. It crunches the data, evaluates millions of flights, and brings you the best deal(s) available. It also indicates the ideal time to fly to your destination. So, if you can shuffle your time a bit, this app will save you some cash.

Gopili — The purpose of the app is to make life easier for travelers and tourists alike. They can book the cheapest seat as long as they are in Europe. Book tickets for coaches, trains, and flights across Europe and it will sort out everything itself. Be it duration, price, or departure time, the app will manage everything for you. Remember to download this before you head over to Europe. The app is available on iOS and Android platforms.

HotelTonight — It is a last-minute hotel booking app, suitable for people whose flight is delayed and need a night or two to crash somewhere. Maybe, staying with the in-laws is not your cup of tea — it doesn't matter — you can still crash using this app. No one wishes to sleep at an airport terminal, so the app saves you from that! The in-app design is elegant and makes it all the easier to locate a hotel in the area. The majority of the listings are discounted, so it doesn't add too much burden on your pocket either. The customer support will help you with suggestions and offer you a way forward to book a room. Don't worry — the app vets all the listings on its app. The app is available on iOS and Android platforms.

Best Transportation Apps

Uber — A huge setback for the regular cab driver industry all over the world, Uber is still the easiest way to get around for anyone. No need to haggle with the local cab drivers over fares or explaining the route. The most accessible route is displayed via Google Maps and that's about it. You just need to pay for the service — credit card and cash are accepted. Uber is available in about 80 countries, making it convenient for you to book it just about anywhere. The app is available on iOS and Android platforms.

Trainline — For the tourists and travelers, this app is quite viable. If you have made plans to visit the UK this year, then you should download this app, pronto. The app has 9.4 million downloads thus far and it remains one of the most highly used transport apps in Britain. The app helps you find upcoming trains and purchase tickets from its virtual counter. You can even get a ticket 10 minutes before the departure, provided that a seat is available. Platform data and live times are also shown on the app, so you can never miss your next train unless you are very careless.

FlightView Free Flight Tracker — The iOS store and Google Play is flooded with flight-status apps, but FlightView stands out from the crowd. For just 99 cents, you get the ad-free version. You can track your flight status and save it for quick access later on. It relays essential information like estimated arrival and departure times if the flight is one time, the gate and terminal numbers for the trip. You can even track the plane via the map (kind of like Careem and Uber). This way, friends and families can track you and arrive on time to pick you from the airport. Neat, isn't it? The app has much more than this. You can look for airports and get information about imminent delays, the weather conditions of the city, a weeklong forecast, as well as map directions. Just like TripIt, you can send your flight details to the app and it will create a trip for you and provide all the required information as well. The app is available on iOS and Android platforms.

Gasbuddy — If you have decided to take a road trip on your vacation, then this app will definitely help you. On a road trip, you may need to refill multiple times, you need to have reliable filling stations at your disposal. So, if you are doing a road trip across Canada and the USA the GasBuddy will walk you through the filling stations along the way. It will also track the cheapest gas stations from the existing ones and list them for you. All the data is user-generated, so the app rewards the users with points for reporting and updating the gas prices. The points make you eligible for free gas and other knockoffs. For the users of electric vehicles, Plugshare is an app that does the same. Apart from showing charging stations on the map, the app has many more useful facilities. Both apps are available on iOS and Android platforms.

Flush Toilet — Yes, there is an app for finding suitable restrooms all over the world. The idea may seem silly, but nothing is more annoying than finding a filthy restroom at a crucial moment. This is where Flush Toilet can save you from that frustration. The app uses location sensors and checks the database of 200,000 public toilets in its registry. It provides other information like fee, key (if necessary), and if the bathroom has facilities for the handicapped. Other than that, another viable feature is that it synchronizes with Google Maps and finds you a suitable restroom even when you are offline. The app is available in iOS and Android platforms.

Yelp! — If your management skills need some brushing up, do not worry. Travelling makes you responsible and warier than before. So, if you have landed in an unfamiliar town and looking to grab a bite, then the Yelp app for you. It has reviews of more than 135 million restaurants all over the world. The reviews are posted by the audience, so you are bound to like something that comes highly recommended. Apart from the audience reviews, you can also check out the menus, book an order, or a reservation for that matter. If you are in a car, then it also lists nearby car services before you get on the road again. The app is available on iOS and Android platforms.

Wi-Fi Finder — As the name suggests, this app can locate the closest Wi-Fi network available. The app has a map that covers the Wi-Fi hotspots in your immediate area and also marks the strongest signal of the lot. Cool, isn't it? The app is presently active in 144 countries. It is available on iOS and Android platforms.

Conclusion

So, there you have it! Your bible for traveling anywhere in the world!

I have researched exhaustively for many months to bring you these insider tips. Besides this, my travels also helped me a lot to put together this book for you. Rest assured, this eBook will always be there for you as a handy reference guide no matter where you are to access it right at your fingertips whenever you need some advice or hacks to make things easier when you're ready for your next trip.

From taking off with the best flight deals, to finding accommodations at great prices, or sailing on amazing cruises at discount fares, you now have the resource that will help you save with ease and discover places around the globe stress-free.

Safe travels!

Index

1

14-day Rule · 83

A

Accommodation Deals · 15

Accommodation Options for Students · 103

Affordable Cruise Options for Solo Travelers and Families · 180

Africa: Live · 171

AirBnb and its Discounts · 60

Airfarewatchdog · 37

Airline Error and Prices · 42

airline search engines · 30

Airlines on Social Media · 72

Alaska during May and September · 186

Algarve, Portugal · 121

Amazon Prime App · 129

Antigua · 168

anti-theft bags · 196

Apps for Europe · 164

Apps for Southeast Asia · 160

ATM Hunter · 133

Austria · 122

Automate Bills · 24

AwardWallet · 132

B

Backpackr · 150

Bahamas Paradise Cruise Lines · 177

Bali · 159

Bar Harbor, Maine · 118

Barcelona, Spain · 121

BonJournal · 174

book in advance · 63

Book your Accommodation · 13

Booking · 14, 43, 47, 51, 54, 58, 59, 62, 74, 179

booking sites · 14

Budget Airlines · 30

Budget Cruise Lines · 177

budget holiday' · 154

Budget Seasons for Cruise Lovers · 186

Buses and Train Discounts · 104

C

Calgary, Canada · 169

Cheap flights · 39

Checklist of Things to Do · 19

Chimani · 134

City Maps 2 Go · 132

Citymapper · 166

CityMaps2Go · 152

Comparison Portals · 66

Cook Islands · 167

Couchsurfing · 55, 152

Country.Hopper · 207

Credit Card Companies · 24

Crowdfund your Trip · 87

Cruise deals · 74

cruise deals on Costco Travel · 76

Cruise in Style for Less · 176

Cruise.com · 179

CruiseComplete.com · 180

D

Discount on Flights for Students · 100

Discounts on Accommodation of Seniors · 111

Disney California Adventure · 120

Disney World Florida · 120

Dosh · 132

Dress Code · 192

Duolingo · 172

E

Eatigo · 161

editing app for free · 153

Educational Trip · 88

Embassy · 191

Emergency Contact Information · 140

Employment as an Au Pair · 95

Expedia · 35

F

Family Vacation Critic · 131

Family Vacation Spots in America · 116

Fareness · 81

Find the Best Airfare · 26

Find Your Park · 130

first rule of packing · 195

Flight Comparison · 44

Flight Discounts for Students · 105

FlightBoard · 80

FlightView Free Flight Tracker · 208

Flush Toilet · 209

Fly Europe · 165

Free Food · 96

Free-of-Charge Flying · 89

Frequency of Your Travelling · 189

frequent flier bonuses · 37

G

Gasbuddy · 209

GateGuru · 210

Gett · 174

Glacier National Park, Montana · 119

Global Freeloaders · 55

GlobeConvert · 161

GMaps · 174

GoEuro · 165

Gogobot · 134

Going Alone · 137

Google Flights · 30

Google Translate · 174

Gopili · 207

Grab · 160

Grand Canyon, Arizona · 119

Grand Circle and Road Scholar · 109

Great Bargains on Overseas Getaways · 154

Greece · 123

H

Healthy Tips for Worry-Free Travel · 188

helpful tips for the budget conscious traveler · 17

Hidden City Ticketing · 41

Hilton Waikoloa Village · 116

Holiday Pirates · 37

Honduras · 169

Honey Chrome Extension · 45

HopStop · 128

Hospitality Club · 55

Hostelbookers · 53

Hostelworld · 162

HotelTonight · 73, 207

How I Earn 1 Million Frequent Flier Miles Every Year · 37

How to Travel Solo · 137

Hudson Valley, New York · 116

I

immunizations · 198

Injury and Illness during the Trip · 190

Ireland · 163

Is Travel Hacking Really a Scam? · 37

J

Jeju Island, South Korea · 157

Jetsetter · 79

K

Kayak · 35

KIDzOUT · 135

L

language barrier · 172

Laos · 158

Last-Minute Deals · 24

Lightroom app · 153

Lodging Apps · 152

Loss of the Money · 189

Loyalty Programs · 92

M

Map Apps · 152

MAPS.ME · 152

Mediterranean in Winter Season · 187

MeetUp.com · 145

Mexico, Bahamas, and Caribbean during Fall Season · 186

Michelin Travel · 166

Momondo · 35

Monument Tracker · 166

Morocco · 171

Mountain hut, Switzerland · 123

Must-download Mobile Apps for Family Vacations · 124

My Disney Experience · 124

My Safetipin · 148

MyTSA · 135

N

Nepal · 156

Never Book on the Weekend · 43

New Delhi, India · 155

Next Flight · 79

Nicaragua · 167

no foreign transaction fee card · 40

North American Belt · 169

Nursing Skills and Free Travel · 87

O

Ocean and River Cruises by Viking · 110

off-season · 29

Older Ships in Mainstream Cruise Lines · 178

One:Night · 78

Onefinestay · 164

OpenTable · 126

Options for Rail · 108

Orbitz · 35

Overall Costs · 12

Overbooked Flight · 93

Overnight Cruises · 183

P

PackPoint Packing List · 129

Park City, UT · 117

Parking Panda · 130

ParkSpotter Africa · 171

Peek · 151

Photo Apps · 153

photo editor tool · 153

planning a trip · 6, 9, 12, 76, 205

Planning Your Trip · 8

Postagram · 125

Prague, Czech Republic · 163

Prepayment · 61

Prescription Medications · 195

Pretty Streets · 165

Priceline · 52

Pro-tips for packing · 22

Provenance · 122

Public Transit · 109

R

RedZone Map · 148, 207

rental car insurance · 18

Rental Options for Seniors · 110

Repositioning Cruises · 184

Ridesharing · 105

Road Accidents · 198

Roadtrippers · 206

Romania · 122

Rome2rio · 206

S

Safeture · 173

Safety Apps for Solo Travelers · 148

San Diego, California · 118

Say no to Single Supplement · 138

Scott's Cheap Flights · 37

Sea for Free · 95

Secret Flying · 37

Seek Local Advice · 191

Selection of Destination · 9

Sit or Squat · 125

Skyscanner · 35

Smart Packing · 21

Snapseed · 127

Social Networking Apps · 150

SoloTraveller · 150

South Africa · 170

Spain · 162

Special Deals · 37

Spotted by Locals · 165

Stress-Free Family Vacations · 112

Student Discounts · 41

Student Discounts Cards · 104

StudentUniverse · 102

sunscreen · 197

Swap Houses · 93

Sygic travel · 206

T

Teach Abroad · 97

Teach English as a Foreign Language · 89

Thailand · 159

The African Belt · 170

The Asian Belt · 155

The Central American Belt · 167

The European Belt · 162

The Flight Deal · 37

The Southeast Asian Belt · 158

The Ultimate Guide to Travel Hacking · 37

TheFork · 166

TheOutbound.com · 152

Three to Four Night Cruises · 183

Tickets in Foreign Currencies · 40

Time of the Trip · 10

Top-6 Holiday Destinations in Europe · 120

Tour and Activity Apps · 151

Tracks and Trails · 131

Trainline · 208

Translation Apps · 149

Transportation · 16

Travel Bloggers · 64

Travel for Free · 86

Travel Insurance · 189

Travel Portals · iii, 2, 5, 7

Travel Scams · 196

traveling companions · 10

Travello · 150

Trekaroo · 130

Trip.com · 78

TripAdvisor · 67, 126

TripCase · 206

TripIt · 127

TripLingo · 167

TripIt · 206

TripWhistle · 148

Trivago · 53

Turkey · 156

U

Undercover Tourist · 133

USA Rest Stops · 128

V

Vacation in Exchange for a Timeshare Presentation · 90

Vacation To Go · 179

Vietnam · 158

Visa Requirements · 21

Vital Documents · 22

VizEat · 149

Vrbo · 84

W

Waze · 128

Weather Underground App · 173

Western Spirit Cycling Adventures · 130

When to Travel · 12

Wi-Fi Finder · 125, 210

Winter Park, Colorado · 118

World Wide Opportunities on Organic Farms · 97

X

XE Currency · 135

XE Currency Converter · 172

Y

Yelp! · 210

Yonder · 150

Yuggler · 124

About the Author

Melvin Harris is the author of several books that showcases practical ideas, valuable references, and savvy tips to help individuals be informed, prepared, and empowered to shop smarter – to live a richer life for less, day after day. He is the founder and CEO of Harris Business Enterprises, LLC whose brands provides consumers who seek good-to-know money-saving insights practical advice on how to buy smart and save time, hassles, and expenses.

For information on eBooks and publications on various topics or to learn more about HBE's products and services, please visit our websites at TPortals.com or HBEShop.com.

About Harris Business Enterprises, LLC

Harris Business Enterprises, LLC (HBE) is a highly-diversified company with interest and expertise in e-commerce, publications, and management consulting. Our mission is to help you prosper and be empowered to live well for less, day after day. Much more than an e-commerce site, we are allies for your quest to save time, save money, and have a stress-free lifestyle to make the most of every day.

For those who are looking to make life easier when they shop, travel, or seek good-to-know money-saving insights, we showcase two go-to websites, TPortals.com and HBEShop.com. It's a destination where savvy consumers can access useful tips, buy smart, be informed, and enhance their experiences.

ABOUT TPORTALS.COM

"INFORMATION THAT EMPOWERS"

TPortals.com (Treasure Portals) delivers publications designed to enrich and educate. It's your gateway to creditable information that helps you be informed, prepared, and empowered. It facilitates you in getting the value you deserve for your hard-earned money. Treasure Portals are resource guides that provide insights and online sources that give you an edge to get things done faster, easier, and smarter. It allows you to free yourself once and for all from the uncertainty and hassles of dealing with unreliable searches and cut through the hype and clutter on the web. Best of all, Treasure Portals guides make it possible for you to live a richer life for less. It showcases simple, readable materials that are filled with practical ideas and valuable references that you can immediately put to use. From e-books that can save you time and money to mini-resource guides that reveal insider tips and shortcuts that you can turn to time and time again. We make it easy for you to obtain valuable information to simplify your life and streamline many of your everyday activities.

ABOUT HBESHOP.COM

"LESS SEARCH, MORE SAVINGS"

HBEShop.com is a marketplace for busy, yet budget-conscious and discerning individuals who relish convenience, value their time, and delight in saving money when shopping for the major brands, services, and stores. Designed for the savvy consumer and bargain hunter who wants to be taken beyond the limits of a particular search category and placed into a broader world that reaches across multiple retail channels that access a variety of products and services without wasting time or energy clicking around the web from website to website. It brings together diverse merchants and organizes them in one convenient place so you can easily find and acquire the things that you need, want, or enjoy. Here a shopper can quickly fulfill their particular purpose first and then delve deeper at their leisure to satisfy an irrepressible appetite for more money-saving opportunities that will certainly be aroused by the immediate sighting of more outstanding products and services, at prices they love. We have teamed up with some of the most respected merchants on the web. These partnerships, along with exclusive HBE products, appeal to every taste, event, and budget for all life's occasions and combine to make you some of the best deals available anywhere.

For information or to learn more about Harris Business Enterprises' products and services, please visit TPortals.com or HBEShop.com or contact us at:

Harris Business Enterprises, LLC

P.O. Pox 3904

Capital Heights, Md. 20971

www.ingramcontent.com/pod-product-compliance
Lightning Source LLC
LaVergne TN
LVHW051400080426
835508LV00022B/2907